THE TROUBLED UNION

THE TROUBLED UNION

Expansionist Imperatives
in Post-Reconstruction
American Novels

JOHN MORÁN GONZÁLEZ

The Ohio State University Press
Columbus

Copyright © 2010 by The Ohio State University.
All rights reserved.

Library of Congress Cataloging-in-Publication Data
González, John Morán.
 The troubled union : expansionist imperatives in
post-reconstruction American novels / John Morán González.
   p. cm.
 Includes bibliographical references and index.
 ISBN-13: 978-0-8142-1129-8 (cloth : alk. paper)
 ISBN-10: 0-8142-1129-1 (cloth : alk. paper)
 ISBN-13: 978-0-8142-9228-0 (cd-rom)
 1. American fiction—19th century—History and criticism. 2. American literature—19th century—History and criticism. 3. National characteristics, American, in literature. 4. Allegory. 5. James, Henry, 1843–1916—Criticism and interpretation. 6. Jackson, Helen Hunt, 1830–1885—Criticism and interpretation. 7. Ruiz de Burton, María Amparo, 1832–1895—Criticism and interpretation. I. Title.
 PS377.G66 2010
 813'.40935873—dc22
                               2010004013
This book is available in the following editions:
Cloth (ISBN 978-0-8142-1129-8)
CD-ROM (ISBN 978-0-8142-9228-0)
Paper (ISBN: 978-0-8142-5636-7)
Cover design by James Baumann
Type set in ITC Century

CONTENTS

Acknowledgments   vii

CHAPTER 1
Introduction:
The Historical Crisis of Post-Reconstruction National Allegory   1

CHAPTER 2
Speaking American:
Henry James and the Dialect of Modernity   21

CHAPTER 3
The Hidden Power:
Domesticity, National Allegory, and Empire in
Helen Hunt Jackson's *Ramona*   50

CHAPTER 4
Blushing Brides and Soulless Corporations:
Racial Formation in María Amparo Ruiz de Burton's
The Squatter and the Don   85

CHAPTER 5
Epilogue:
Decentering National Allegory   107

Notes   113
Works Cited   130
Index   136

ACKNOWLEDGMENTS

Upon learning that I spent my childhood in the Texas border town of Brownsville, many people comment upon my apparent lack of an accent, claiming that I don't sound like a Texan. Apparently, I frustrated their expectation that my voice would provide a legible personal history. Like the Armenian migrant questioned by Henry James at the turn of the last century, I find myself the subject of categorical confusion in terms of ethnicity. My fair complexion, dark eyes, wavy hair, and middle-class mannerisms make my social background interestingly ambiguous. However, I have little doubt that what speakers of "standard English" would call my mother's Spanish accent would immediately place her as a recent Mexican immigrant even though she was born a U.S. citizen. On her lap and on my father's knee, I learned Midwestern-inflected English and border Mexican Spanish, creating a little social chaos in their intersection.

These conversations have often taken place far from the geopolitical borderlands of the United States and Mexico, but differences of other sorts from the East Coast to the West, from Texas to the Midwest, have made imagining this project possible. The surprising links between these places have as well. I would foremost like to thank my dissertation adviser at Stanford University, Professor Ramón Saldívar. His example, as a scholar and teacher sets the tone. My deepest appreciation extends to the other members of my committee, Jay Fliegelman and Al Gelpi. I would also like to acknowledge two unofficial members of my dissertation committee, Lora Romero and Susan Gillman, who gave great advice and support.

I would also like to thank the members of my dissertation-reading group: Carrie Bramen, David Cantrell, and Eric Schocket were particularly constructive critics and even better friends. A special thanks goes to Josie Saldaña and Inés Salazar, who adopted me when I entered graduate school and guided me past its perils.

A portion of chapter 3 was previously published as "The Warp of Whiteness: Domesticity and Empire in Helen Hunt Jackson's *Ramona*," in *American Literary History* 16:3 (Fall 2004): 437–65. A portion of chapter 4 was previously published as "The Whiteness of the Blush: The Cultural Politics of Racial Formation in *The Squatter and the Don*," in *María Amparo Ruiz de Burton: Critical and Pedagogical Perspectives*, eds. Amelia María de la Luz Montez and Anne E. Goldman (Lincoln: University of Nebraska Press, 2004), 153–68. I am grateful to Oxford University Press and the University of Nebraska Press for granting permission for the publication of this material.

I wish to acknowledge the Mellon Foundation, the Ford Foundation, and the Stanford Humanities Center for their financial support during the completion of this project.

A list hardly does justice to the organic sense of community built over time, but let me thank those who have made surviving academia possible: Frances Aparicio, Betty Bell, Alicia Schmidt-Camacho, Elaine Chang, Maria Cotera, Dionne Espinoza, Dane Johnson, Marcia Klotz, Rob Latham, Tiffany Ana López, Lee Medavoi, Diane Nelson, Steve Pitti, Margo Ponce, Brian Rourke, Xiomara Santamarina, and Lucia Suarez. Cynthia Williams, Andrea Torrice, Don McLean and the Lorax group get special acknowledgment for constantly reminding me not all intelligent life resides in academia.

I'd like to thank my colleagues in the Department of English, the Center for Mexican American Studies, and the Department of American Studies at the University of Texas at Austin: Phil Barrish, Brian Bremen, Evan Carton, Oscar Casares, James Cox, Ann Cvetkovich, John McKiernan González, Rolando Hinojosa-Smith, Steve Hoelscher, Meta Jones, Martin Kevorkian, Julia Lee, Gretchen Murphy, Domino Perez, Jennifer Wilks, and Emilio Zamora. A special thanks goes to José E. Limón for his brilliant mentorship.

The folks at The Ohio State University Press have been fantastic to work with. I would especially like to thank Sandy Crooms and Eugene O'Connor for nurturing this book to fruition. I owe Linda Webster a brace of thanks for indexing this book and my previous one. A generous University Co-operative Society Subvention Grant awarded by the University of Texas at Austin helped bring this publication to print. A special thanks goes to Stephanie Boydell and the Special Collections division of the Sir

Kenneth Green Library at Manchester Metropolitan University for providing the splendid Walter Crane cover art.

On a more personal note, this book would have never been written without the persistent support of my family: Paul and Mari González, Mónica González, Pedro and Angelita García, Pamela and Joey Delgado, Kit and Leslie Ashby. Uncle John sends much love to Lynn, Pierce, and Lillian Ashby and Paul Delgado, as well as to Pablo Abiel, José Cáleb, and Monica Lucero González. Finally, my wife, Patricia Marie García, has been interlocutor, editor, and advisor throughout the publication process. Together with our daughter Angelita "Tita," you make all things possible through your love.

In the experience of writing this book, I hear my parents' voices echo in the passages of text I have written. That echo has moved me, at times only half-conscious of the influence, into matters of nationalism and literary form in the context of the late nineteenth-century United States. Their voices stand, not as guards but as guides, at the borders of a multitude of lived experiences in the United States: migration, citizenship, cultural difference, and diaspora. I dedicate these pages to them, Juan y Matiana González.

CHAPTER 1

Introduction

The Historical Crisis
of Post-Reconstruction
National Allegory

> Love had set himself a hard task. He had set before him this problem: "New England Puritanism and Southern Prejudice; how shall they be reconciled?"
> —Albion Tourgée, *Bricks Without Straw* (1880)

> Ruins, to be interesting, have to be massive.
> —Henry James, *The American Scene* (1907)

In the final chapter of Mark Twain's 1885 novel *The Adventures of Huckleberry Finn*, Huck itches to "light out for the [Indian] Territory," heading west "ahead of the rest." Leaving behind the undercivilized ex-slave Jim and the overcivilized, watch-minding Tom Sawyer, Huck anticipates displacing his recently completed North-South journey upon the Mississippi River with an East-West trajectory that promises "howling adventures amongst the Injuns" (321). This change of direction is also a change of purpose, one that suggests a national reorientation away from the divisive North-South travails of Reconstruction and a resumption of a familiar narrative of imperialist nation building along an East-West axis. While Frederick Jackson Turner's essay "The Significance of the Frontier in American History" most succinctly expressed this metaphoric reorientation in 1893, many novels of national reconciliation from the 1880s to the turn of the twentieth century forged the sense that the United States would reunite as a white nation by returning to the imperial expansionism of its pre–Civil War past.

Huckleberry Finn, set forty to fifty years before its 1885 publication date, is a national allegory detailing the post-Reconstruction plight of the unfree freedmen. The novel, particularly its troubling final chapters, plays out the paradox of the Jim Crow re-enslavement of legally freed ex-slaves. Yet Indian Territory was also new around 1840, having been organized by Congress in the 1834 Indian Trade and Intercourse Act. Anticipating the removal of the Cherokee and other southeastern tribal nations, President Andrew Jackson and Congress enacted a key colonial management policy integral to the development of Manifest Destiny, along whose westward path of empire Huck gleefully trips. Like the eponymous protagonist, *Huckleberry Finn* exchanges the harrowing post-Reconstruction politics of setting "a free nigger free" for the apparently less problematic imperial project of experiencing frontier life "over in the Territory" (318; 321).

Ultimately, the narrative identifies a North-South orientation with the insoluble domestic problem of white supremacy, while a ludic nation-building imperialism distinguishes the East-West axis. Populated by Indians whose racial differences did not play into the divisive national trauma of slavery and its aftermath, Indian Territory becomes the figurative grounds upon which *Huckleberry Finn* can restore the nation's imperial narrative so rudely interrupted by the Civil War and Reconstruction. Proleptically substituting the imperial burden of conquering and civilizing savages for the national problem of enforcing civil rights, the novel's ending suggests that imperial expeditions out West rather than civil rights down South would succeed in rejoining the sundered sections of the nation divided over the fate of the freedmen.[1]

This nexus of sectional conflict, national history, and narrative form in *Huckleberry Finn* hints at the complex cultural resignification of U.S. identity following the end of Reconstruction. Over the following three decades, literature, particularly the historical romance, played a vital role in metonymically remapping questions of racial signification onto a national topography. The thorny problem of remaking a nation out of North and South would find its solution in imperial nation building out West. This proposition may seem surprising, given that the 1880s, the decade I consider most closely in this study, has not usually been interpreted as one of the key moments in U.S. imperialist maneuverings. Situated roughly halfway between the much-studied military conquests of 1848 and 1898, the early post-Reconstruction period has been more typically interpreted as expressing the cultural anxieties of a national, domestic nature: the reunification of North and South, the white supremacist implementation of Jim Crow, the industrial development of monopoly capitalism, the rise of class strife in the land of free labor, the growing impact of immigration upon national identity, the advent of the "New Woman," and the final conquest of tribal nations.

Yet, as my reading of *Huckleberry Finn* suggests, I wish to emphasize the importance of literature in maintaining an imperialist disposition within U.S. civil society even when the actual moments of imperialist aggression lay generations in the past (or in the future).[2] I foreground the utmost centrality of that disposition to the making of U.S. nationality during those interstitial moments through public and domestic literary discourses.[3] Literature has been a key site of examination for recent studies of the cultures of U.S. imperialism, not least of all because of its key role in forming modern subjectivities.[4] As Amy Kaplan and Lora Romero have suggested in their respective studies of the antebellum domestic novel, print culture mediated the formation of imperialist subjectivities in complex, often contradictory manners, yet nonetheless provided the cultural justifications for Manifest Destiny.[5] For the post-Reconstruction period, Kaplan, Bill Brown, and others have examined westerns, adventure narratives, and the nascent genre of science fiction for the formation of imperialist white masculinity.[6]

My own focus is the post-Reconstruction historical romance, particularly the subgenre known as "the romance of reunion." Often explicitly operating as a national allegory of reunion, the historical romance of this period traces the uneven development of this imperial sense of national identity through courtship and marriage plots. With the task of "civilizing" savages more appealing than addressing the savage racial inequalities of U.S. civilization, the post-Reconstruction historical romance itself migrates from Henry James's Boston to the terminus of antebellum Manifest Destiny, California. Focusing on the directional vacillations of post-Reconstruction national allegory, my project involves examining the cultural work of the historical romance in outlining the imperial formation of U.S. nationalism from the end of Reconstruction in 1877 until the publication of James's travel narrative *The American Scene* in 1907. The historical romances that I most closely consider—James's *The Bostonians* (1886), Helen Hunt Jackson's *Ramona* (1884), María Amparo Ruiz de Burton's *The Squatter and the Don* (1885)—trace the vexed project of forging a national identity during the pivotal decade of the 1880s, after the end of Reconstruction but before the complete codification of Jim Crow.

Symptomatically displaying the national crisis of destabilized gender, racial, and class differences, these historical romances restabilized national identity through a revived sense of imperial destiny. The submerged sense that national reunion could only take place through the imperial imagination—whether actualized or not—underwrites overt literary attempts to foster reconciliation between North and South. Through the romance of reunion, the United States would rebuild its own sense of national identity by revamping its imperial legacy for the future.

The Cultural Persistence of Empire

The two major moments of imperial expansion prior to the Civil War—the Louisiana Purchase and U.S.-Mexican War—defined U.S. national identity well beyond their immediate moments. The cultural persistence of imperialist thought into the post-Reconstruction era stemmed from the antebellum configuration of national identity in which sectional differences were mitigated by imperial expansion. Before the Civil War, North and South were the primary topographical metaphors for the sometimes conflictual, usually synergistic ensemble of free and slave labor that propelled Manifest Destiny. After Reconstruction, North and South did not so much disappear as distinct cultural regions of the United States but rather became subsumed under renovated practices of imperialism figured as the new sense of empire. Generating and fulfilling a national narrative of Manifest Destiny, the formal annexation of new territories marked only the first phase of the settler colonialism that characterized U.S. nineteenth-century nation building.

The subjugation of tribal nations remained a constant activity throughout the years between imperial acquisitions, furnishing the adventure narratives, ethnographic accounts, and other racialist discourses of empire that nurtured U.S. imperialist subjectivities. Forming national identity through the colonial tropes of Indian savagery, Mexican semi-barbarism and black slavery, the narrative of Manifest Destiny and the narrative of North and South formed a kind of ideological chiasmus through which the nation could be imagined as both free and slave simultaneously. The debates over the extension of slavery into newly annexed territories resulted in federal legislation, from the Northwest Ordinance of 1787 until the Compromise of 1850, which reaffirmed North and South as distinct economic and cultural regions while uniting these sections as one in the nation-building enterprise of imperial expansion.

The acquisition of Mexico's northern half in 1848 accomplished Manifest Destiny's goal of a continental empire spanning from the Atlantic Ocean to the Pacific, but it also brought about the national crisis that the

Compromise of 1850 was crafted to avoid. The Civil War and Reconstruction disrupted the unifying national narrative of Manifest Destiny, precipitating a crisis of national identity as well as in national politics. During the 1850s, the national narrative became the sectional conflict between North and South centered upon slavery, in effect upsetting what had been the delicate national balance of embarking upon new imperial conquests while managing older, more settled colonial acquisitions. What remained was a profound political disjuncture between regional modes of labor exploitation that resulted in the Civil War. In effect, the Civil War interrupted the antebellum narrative of continental conquest and settlement that had provided the ideological grounds of nationhood, leaving the nation bereft of a unifying historical destiny. Reconstruction further divided the nation as Southern whites reasserted white supremacy over the region through a campaign of terror—marked by the lynching of black men and the rape of black women—against the freedmen's civil rights.

Post-Reconstruction National Allegory

The withdrawal of federal troops from the former Confederate states in 1877 marked the end of Reconstruction and the triumph of white supremacy. But even if the freedmen were sacrificed for the sake of ending the protracted civil conflict, the sense of nationhood remained in tatters. Print culture could heal past national wounds, according to prominent men of letters who promoted national reconciliation through the nation's middle-class literary magazines and novels. Reviewing George Washington Cable's historical romance *The Grandissimes* for serialization in 1878, *Century Magazine* editor Richard Gilder commented, "[T]he book will accomplish something, no doubt, to bring about the days of better understanding and more cordial feeling" (qtd. in Kreyling xiii). Gilder would later initiate a long-running series of Civil War campaign reminisces by both Union and Confederate soldiers that overlapped with the serial run of Henry James's *The Bostonians* in the same magazine.[7] Emerging during the 1870s and 1880s to imaginatively refuse the split halves of the nation, the romance of reunion became something of a national habit, a practice of reading and writing that defined what the nation should be. In tandem with the sectional reconciliation rehearsed in national print culture, commemorations and monuments of the Civil War increasingly paid tribute to the fallen soldiers on both sides throughout the 1870s and 1880s.

These two aspects of the culture of national reunion converge in *The*

Bostonians as Southerner Basil Ransom and Yankee Verena Tarrant pay a visit to Harvard University's Memorial Hall. Completed in 1878, the "ornate, overtopping structure" reminds Ransom of "the simple emotion of the old fighting-time," a sentiment that makes him forget "the whole question of sides and parties." Although dedicated to Harvard students and alumni who had died fighting for the Union, "the finest piece of architecture he had ever seen" bears no reproach for the ex-Confederate Ransom; rather, "the monument around him seemed an embodiment of that memory" that "arched over friends as well as enemies, the victims of defeat as well as the sons of triumph" (225). Downplaying the bitter political divisions and fratricidal bloodshed, the widespread campaign for sectional reconciliation instead presented the experiences of former combatants on both sides as part of one national experience.[8]

Likewise enticing the reader to forget the past, the romance of reunion dissolved contentious sectional politics in wedded bliss. As Nina Silber's study *The Romance of Reunion* extensively documents, scores of romance of reunion novels between 1865 and the turn of the century depicted North and South setting aside sectional differences in order to reunite as one nation. Historical romances such as John DeForest's *The Bloody Chasm* (1881), Julia Magruder's *Across the Chasm* (1885), Opie Read's *A Kentucky Colonel* (1889), E. P. Roe's *Miss Lou* (1888), Stephen T. Robinson's *The Shadow of the War* (1884), James S. Rogers's *In Our Regiment* (1884), Maud Howe Elliott's *Atalanta in the South* (1886), John Habberton's *Brueton's Bayou* (1886), and Charles King's *Kitty's Conquest* (1884) and *A War-Time Wooing* (1888) figured heterosexual romantic love as the model of national consensus. The romance of reunion employed a sentimentalized aesthetics of nation building in order to imagine a new United States in which the freedmen had only subordinate roles. Typically the courtship took place between a Southern white woman and a Northern white man, usually a soldier or businessman. Spiteful disdain gives way to heartfelt romance as the Southern woman relinquished her Confederate sympathies and slave-power politics for Yankee love and domestic bliss. Explicitly operating as a national allegory, the romance of reunion appealed to the sentimental heart that forgave and sympathized rather than to the political head that schemed and legislated.[9] Reimagining the Union as the consensual marital coupling of former enemies, the romance of reunion provided a popular way to naturalize the contentious processes of national reunification by refiguring the South's clearly subordinated political status as the wife's dutiful place within an apparently depoliticized hierarchy of patriarchal gender relations. As Silber has noted, womanly consent to marriage legitimated the exercise of masculine Northern authority in economic and political matters.

The ever-present fact of Northern military, economic, and political power over the South may have been legitimated under the sign of marriage, but even this homology between regions and spouses left the South-as-blushing-bride a realm of relative autonomy within her own sphere. The masculine North might exercise authority in national leadership but also allowed the feminized South to tend to its domestic affairs of racial segregation. Positing a national division of labor modeled upon the patriarchal division of labor, the romance of reunion articulated the racialist logic of home rule that led to the codification of Jim Crow. By the turn of the century, the domestic logic of the romance of reunion would come to figure the imperial logic of U.S. nationalism by suggesting that white nations are born, and not made, of white Northern and Southern parents.

The Success of Post-Reconstruction National Allegory

Collapsing any distinction between the making of white families and the making of the white nation, the post-Reconstruction romance of reunion reached its zenith in Thomas Dixon's 1905 novel *The Clansman*. In its closing passage, white love and white politics unite as Ku Klux Klan Grand Dragon Ben Cameron celebrates the Klan's *coup d'état* with fiancée Elsie Stoneman. Linking her desire to start a white family with Ben's desire for white supremacy, Elsie tells her lover, "Your fate hangs in the balance of this election tonight. . . . I'll share it with you, success or failure, life or death" (374). Love and politics mix inextricably in this second novel of Dixon's Klan Trilogy, merging sexual desire and white supremacy to make the personal quite political; indeed, the fulfillment of the former is predicated upon the enactment of the latter. The converse is also true: the Knights of the Invisible Empire ride not only for "their God" and "their land" but mainly for the "white womanhood of the South" (338). Making those desires one and the same, *The Clansman* marks the moment at the turn of the century when the reconsolidation of U.S. nationalism around whiteness crystallizes into the epitome of the post-Reconstruction national allegory.

Subtitled "A Historical Romance of the Ku Klux Klan," *The Clansman*, like other romances of reunion, joins the white North and white South, previously sundered by the Civil War and Radical Reconstruction, through the marriages between the children of a Northern abolitionist senator and the children of a patrician ex-slaveholder. In representing the white families of North and South as uniting to overthrow the alleged "black misrule" of Reconstruction, *The Clansman* translates the political differences of section between whites into the spiritual differences of race and citizenship between black and white, as Walter Benn Michaels has argued. In granting nationality something of the ontology of race, the novel transforms the African Americans of the federal army and the state legislature into the occupying forces of a racial empire against whose imperial domination whites struggle to give birth to a constitutional republic.[10] With the greatness of this "Republic" identified with the "the genius of the race of pioneer white freemen who settled this continent," *The Clansman* makes "the purity of this racial stock" the guarantee of white "Civilization" over mongrel multiracial "Democracy" (291).

Linking imperial destiny to white women's bodies performs the cultural work of making the white patriarchal family the paradigm of white nationhood; hence the novel's equation of the Redemption of the South with the redemption of white womanhood, "the divinity that claimed and received the chief worship of man" (210). The Klan's ride to overthrow Reconstruction's black misrule is justified not so much by malicious and incompetent management of governmental offices (already illegal and illegitimate in any case within the novel's logic) as by the fabricated threat of black men's violent sexual access to the bodies of white women. In this sense, citizenship in the nation, white by definition, is secured as much by the policing of white women's sexuality as by the castration and lynching of black males. If the novel obliterates the more general fact of black women's experiences of sexual coercion by white men before and after Emancipation, then this erasure serves to legitimate marriage as the proper mode of white men's access to white women's bodies in cementing North and South along the color line.[11]

Joined to this legal sexual access is the sexual division of labor central to this reconfiguration of nation around race in *The Clansman*. Michaels makes the lucid suggestion that the Klan's white sheets, "far from making [individual clansmen's] visible identities invisible," render "invisible identities visible" ("Souls of White Folk" 190). But this revelation is enabled only through the work of white women, whose presence in the making of white nationalism is not merely an alibi for the demonizing of African American males but rather fundamental to the structuring of white nationalist desire. Sewing together the white sheets that make white souls visible, the wives, sisters, and daughters of the white South make, and make visible, the ghostly trappings of the Invisible Empire, thereby highlighting their own silent role in founding the white nation: "Over four hundred thousand [Klan] disguises for men and horses were made by the women of the South, and not one secret ever passed their lips!" (343). Home work makes the Invisible Empire work; the Klan's women-made sheets serve as the nationalist flag of white supremacy.

After the white nationalist revolution, what white men have won white women must continue in the work of the family. The task of maintaining the affective ties of nation is represented as women's work, as a normalized domestic bliss maintained after the heroic white masculinist triumph over political and other obstacles to national unity. The labor of white women enables the new dominant configuration of racialized national identity across political, class, and other differences among Southern whites not only by making white national identity ("souls") visible but also by making that identity generally available. As such, domestic labor transformed what had been the antebellum planter class's privileged ownership of particular slaves into any white man's post-Reconstruction police power and material privileges over all African Americans. The nationalist economy of *The Clansman* thus articulates not only a racialist nationalism in which only whites are citizens but also reinscribes a gendered division of access, influence, and agency within the public and private spheres of the nation.[12]

With the birth of the white nation accomplished, *The Clansman* would project the new U.S. imperialism of 1898 from the vantage point of Redemption. Signaling this "American Revolution," Dixon gave the four subsections of *The Clansman* titles that allude to the establishment of France as the first modern European nation. Loosely following the phases of the French Revolution, those subsection titles are "The Assassination," "The Revolution," "The Reign of Terror," and finally, "The Ku Klux Klan." If the "Klan" section embodies the restoration of a proper racial order in the founding of the white U.S. nation, then it also makes visible the imperial trajectory of the nation by suggesting that, like the imperial First Empire that followed the French Revolution, what comes after Redemption are U.S. incursions into racial empires of the nonwhite regions of the globe. This trajectory suggests the imperative of imperial expansion hinted at in the subtitle of the first Klan Trilogy novel, *The Leopard's Spots*: "A Romance of the White Man's Burden." Thus, what Michaels calls "anti-imperialist" novels can explicitly legitimate the imperialist ventures of the United States during and after the U.S.-Spanish War.

Foundational Fictions: The U.S. Exception

If *The Clansman* represents the zenith of the racial restructuring of national allegory in the post-Reconstruction period, it also bears an anomalous relationship to the U.S. canon. Although a bestseller when published at the turn of the century, the novel has subsequently been viewed as a sociological relic, lacking any aesthetic merit, from cruder days of racialist thought. Indeed, virtually none of the novels that Silber analyses in her extensive study can be considered canonical. Unlike the Latin American foundational fictions studied by Doris Sommer, the heterosexual, middle-class family romance failed to become, in any canonical way, the foundational fiction of the United States.[13] Insofar as the United States shares the dynamics of settler colonialism and Creole revolutionary nationalism with other American nations, then U.S. canonical history of national allegory bears family resemblances, as it were, to other American national novels.[14] Within the divergences of local histories lie the differences of form that national allegory would take in each nation; the sustained history of U.S. imperialist expansion throughout the nineteenth century results in the unique problem (for the Americas) of nation building through imperialism.

The U.S. canonical novel for the most part revolves around male camaraderie, or what Benedict Anderson has termed the "perverse, eroticized brotherhood of nationalism" ("Holy Perversions" 9). James Fennimore Cooper's Chingachgook and Natty Bumpo, Herman Melville's Queequeg and Ishmael, and Mark Twain's Huck Finn and Jim exemplify the interracial, homosocial pairings that Anderson finds characteristic of U.S. canonical novels. Pairing white and nonwhite men, these homosocial narratives have until recently defined the aesthetic contours of U.S. literary studies. These interracial duos literally embody the extent of U.S. imperial expansions; an Indian, a Polynesian, and an African American are respectively matched to a white man. To the extent that these homosocial narratives have been canonized as national allegories, they also demonstrate the limits of imagining national unity through consensual heterosexual romances. Recourse to eroticized fraternity makes narrative closure by the domestic bliss of reproductive marriage difficult at best.[15]

Other texts seem to reinforce this sense even if heterosexual and procreative. The U.S. nineteenth-century novel, of which Nathaniel Hawthorne's dysfunctional family narrative *The Scarlet Letter* is exemplary and James's *The Bostonians* a close relative, proves a less than ideal basis for founding the nation along the more apparently stable lines of the Latin American paradigm. Sommer's "peculiarly American" becomes in Anderson's idiom the "peculiar 'American' institution," hinting at the trajectory of his comments upon the U.S. exceptionalism to the Creole, heterosexual historical romance of the Americas. According to Anderson, the canonical novels of the United States could not represent the national reconciliation of whites and their racial others through an eroticized, vaguely incestuous marriage of national brothers and sisters. The sexual nature of white men's violent colonial exploitation of nonwhite women, as witnessed by large mestizo and mulatto populations, prohibited the national incorporation of indigenous and African peoples even figuratively in the face of remembered wrongs.

For those American nations where the Creole or *criollo* revolutionaries were also slaveholders unwilling to abolish slavery in the course of national liberation, it was impossible to imagine national communities linked by cross-racial, heterosexual marriage.[16] If for Sommer the cultural work of the historical romance was to unite the various classes, races, and regions of the nation through notions of mutual attraction and procreative sexuality guaranteed by the state, then for Anderson the prolonged, violent sexual exploitation of nonwhite women, particularly black women, would constrain the very structure of national allegory in the Americas.[17] The U.S. foundational fiction could not, then, be imagined by its elites as uniting the nation when the state itself had sanctioned such racialized sexual violence. The all-too-evident and literal fraternity enacted through racialized sexual coercion would make narrating national unity across color lines very nearly unthinkable, even if political developments such as the abolition of slavery had created a multiracial citizenry.

In the face of such deep social rifts, only the allegorical imaginings of a non-reproductive homosociality would enable dominant representations of colonizing white men and colonized men of color. Circumventing the perils of paternity and culpability, U.S. canonical novels could unite the nation fraternally while erasing the primal scene of colonial exploitation. The narrative solution to the social problem of racialized sexual exploitation reveals the limits of imagining nation in this way, insofar as these interracial, homosocial pairings almost never survive the narrative.

Queequeg dies battling the White Whale, while Huck finds himself itching to "light out for the Territory" without Jim. Chingachgook and Natty Bumpo may grow old together, but the death of Chingachgook's only child, Uncas (significantly a son and not a daughter), in *The Last of the Mohicans* foretells the future impossibility of such nationalized, racially mixed male couples. In this sense, canonical U.S. national allegories can be considered as failures in their inability to project national unity into the future. Like the other white survivors of these colonial homosocial pairings, only Ishmael lives to tell the tale of U.S. nationhood.

The Failure of Post-Reconstruction National Allegory

The post–Civil War romance of reunion did emphasize heterosexual romantic union as the basis for national unification, but the imperial legacies that underwrite their successes in imagining a white nation undermined that very possibility. The romance of reunion began the 1880s with marital bliss and ended the decade in martial bloodshed. This difference in narrative possibilities between George Washington Cable's historical romance *The Grandissimes* and Mark Twain's historical novel *A Connecticut Yankee at King Arthur's Court* not only highlights Cable's relative optimism at the end of the 1870s and Twain's certain pessimism at the end of the 1880s but also their underpinnings by the U.S. imperialist imaginary. Both novels turn to the past as allegorized settings of the Reconstruction-era South: the Louisiana Purchase of 1803, as experienced in Creole New Orleans, in the case of the former, and sixth-century England in the latter's case. If Cable could imagine a happy albeit contested conclusion to the terms of national reunion at the dawn of the 1880s, then by the end of the decade Twain would highlight the seeming impossibility of such a project altogether.

First serialized in *Scribner's Monthly* from November 1879 until October of the following year, *The Grandissimes* celebrates the rocky yet ultimately consensual merging of Creole Louisiana into the Union after "the Cession." The narrative symbolizes this consensus through the wedded unions of enemies old and new. In the novel's closing chapter, Creole Honoré Grandissime wins the hand of Creole belle Aurore Nancanou, widow of the scion of his family's old clan rivals, the De Grapions. Rejecting the old Southern codes of honor that widowed Aurore when her husband lost a dual with his uncle, Honoré atones for his family's questionable dispossession of the widow and her daughter Clotilde by returning to them the title to the De Grapion plantation. Risking his family's economic ruin yet compelled by his moral vision to act justly, Honoré proves his moral fitness for marriage to Aurore by first restoring the Nancanous' financial independence and then openly acknowledging the quadroon half-brother (the "f.m.c.") who shares his name but not his whiteness. Working for racial equality despite his family's ire, Honoré finds his reward in Aurore's arms as she finally "let him clasp her to his bosom" (339). Burying the South's past of racial prejudice as well as the chivalric code of honor that perpetrated senseless violence among its leading families, the union of Honoré and Aurore prepares the way for a New South more devoted to modern notions of racial equality and to the honest industry of commerce.

Anticipating New Orleans to become, thanks to the Mississippi River, the great trade hub between the Caribbean and the expected U.S. settlements of the continental interior, Honoré Grandissime and Northern immigrant Joseph Frowenfeld invest in the westward expansion of the United States already initiated by the Lewis and Clark Expedition. Their commercial activity represents the modern antithesis of the old Creole code of honor that shunned trade as unworthy of proper gentlemen. But as the novel makes clear, their financial acumen spearheads the political rationalization of national incorporation. Frowenfeld, a German-American immigrant from Philadelphia, represents the Northern reformer whose ideas of formal equality are harshly questioned by the hostile Creoles. Figured as a kind of Yankee carpetbagger who sets down roots in New Orleans as an apothecary, "Professor" Frowenfeld finds his firm beliefs in the Enlightenment discourses of reason, laissez faire capitalism, and civic equality scarcely tested by the passionate Creoles.

Rather, the "barbaric" and "feline" beauty of Palmyre Philosophe tempts Frowenfeld to collapse the key liberal distinction between public civil rights and private social association (71).[18] Nearly seduced by this quadroon mistress of "voudou" and intimate of Aurore, Frowenfeld scarcely avoids "compromise," the danger that transplanted white Northerners, rather than challenge the South's invidious racial hierarchies, would all-too-readily "acclimate" to them (37). Finding Palmyre's very touch "poisonous" to his reason, Frowenfeld finds his principles compromised by his racialized sexual desire (201). Only his as-yet unrealized love for Clotilde Nancanou saves the "pure white within" from a mad descent into "the shadow of the Ethiopian" (204; 156). Frowenfeld's economic partnership with the level-headed, principled Clotilde, followed by marriage to her, rationalizes the Union's economic and political reintegration even while avoiding the dangers of social equality with those to whom political equality has been extended. If Honoré and Aurore represent the reformation of the old South into post-Reconstruction commercial modernity, then the union of Frowenfeld and Clotilde signals the new national unity achieved through such modernization.

The Grandissimes offers no such happy union for the freedmen. Palmyre Philosophe, equivocally consumed by her unrequited love for the white Honoré Grandissime and by her desire for revenge upon the entire white race, spurns the love of the nonwhite Honoré Grandissime. Philosophe and the f.m.c. eventually journey to France to work out their relationship, yet this transaction only involves the exchange of money and not of vows; a snooping sea captain concludes, "He wants to charter her . . . but she doesn't like his rates" (330). But Palmyre truly desires not wealth but whiteness, even as she seeks to destroy it. Similarly, Honoré desires what he cannot attain: the ability to shed the racial mark of the initials f.m.c. Driven to despair by his ironic, supplementary status, the "not quite/not white" Honoré Grandissime commits suicide after bequeathing all his wealth to the *femme fatale* Philosophe, who chooses to remain in Bordeaux (Bhabha 92). Dangerous yet ineffectual, obsessive rather than rational, the freedmen have no place within Cable's desiring economy of nationhood. Linking the failure to realize a lasting relationship to their obsession with the social equality they can never attain, *The Grandissimes* exiles the freedmen from the narrative of the post-Reconstruction nation.

Yet the racialized exclusion of the freedmen from the nation is less a failure of Cable's liberalism than a trace of the imperial ideologies structuring this tale of national unification. In allegorizing the South as the Louisiana Purchase, and the question of national reunion as one of imperial acquisition, *The Grandissimes* casts the opposition to this incorporation as the resistance of "the whole tribe of Grandissime" (316). If Frowenfeld and Honoré Grandissime join to support freedmen's rights and national reunion, then the greatest threat comes from Honoré's uncle Agricola Fusilier, whose own Indian blood becomes reified as the source of his, and his "tribe's," opposition to "the Américain invader" (157). Considered by Dr. Keene as the degenerate evolutionary equivalent of "an orangoutang," the reactionary Citizen Agricola nonetheless demands "his lands, his rights and the purity of his race" (101; 283). Refusing to acknowledge kinship with his relative Honoré Grandissime, f.m.c., on the basis of white supremacy's horror of miscegenation with blacks, Agricola proudly touts his own mixed ancestry as a descendent of the "Indian princess" Lufki-Humma.

Although depicted as barbaric as the enslaved African prince Bras-Coupé, "Agricola's most boasted ancestor" only a few generations removed does not qualify Agricola's "right to smite the fairest and most distant descendant of an African on the face" because "the darkness of her cheek had no effect to make him less white" (18). Figuring Agricola as a kind of white Indian, and therefore the epitome of the unreconstructed white Southerner, *The Grandissimes* invokes the racialist logic of imperialist nation building that demands either the death or removal of such obstacles. Indeed, the two racial problems of the novel solve each other as Honoré Grandissime, f.m.c., kills Agricola in retaliation for years of racial humiliation. Even as the text casts this event as poetic justice, nonetheless this event prompts the f.m.c.'s short-lived, ill-fated exile in France with Palmyre Philosophe. With North and South cast onto the westward path of empire, the two white couples can maintain the nation's racial purity in carrying out their common imperial project while guiltlessly becoming free of the disturbing presence of either white African Americans or white Indians.

In *The Grandissimes*, Cable suggested that "two great forces" could ultimately make Southern white acceptance of the freedmen's civil rights a reality: "Religion and Education" (95). Seeking to educate the public as well as make some money, Cable joined Twain on a four-month speaking tour in late 1884 and early 1885 as fellow novelists advocating racial equality and civil rights. Just before his polemical essay against Jim Crow, "The Freedmen's Case in Equity," appeared in the January 1885 issue of the *Century Magazine*, Cable introduced Malory's *Morte D'Arthur* to his podium partner. Twain later acknowledged Cable as the source of inspiration for *A Connecticut Yankee at King Arthur's Court*, yet came to a radically different conclusion about the possibility of national reconciliation upon terms that still upheld the civil rights of freedmen. In 1880, *The Grandissimes* could still envision a North and South united on some uncompromised version of the North's terms. By the time *A Connecticut Yankee* was published in late 1889, what appeared to Cable as the distinct probability of national reunification through imperial imaginings became in Twain's narrative a fragile but dangerous illusion that "merely modified savages" would willingly accept modernist reconstruction (125).

Like the unreconstructed Creoles of *The Grandissimes*, the Britons of sixth-century England were mostly "white Indians," according to Hank

Morgan, the time-traveling protagonist of Twain's *A Connecticut Yankee* (53). An awkward interloper in a strange, backwards land, Morgan is, much like Frowenfeld, "a Yankee of the Yankees," intensely "practical" and "nearly barren of sentiment . . . or poetry" (36). In the footsteps of his namesake, the anthropologist Lewis Henry Morgan (himself a New York Yankee), the Connecticut Yankee provides a detailed ethnographic account of a barbaric Camelot and its "sort of polished-up court of Comanches" (138). Seeking to advance Britain's clock of cultural evolution from barbarism to civilization, Morgan, who assumes the very nineteenth-century title of "Sir Boss," sets out to modernize the medieval world by introducing nineteenth-century industrial technology and democratic institutions, including an end to slavery and universal suffrage.[19] Echoing the Northern opinion that the South needed to fully institute capitalist relations of wage labor in order to displace the previous dependency upon slavery, industrial development becomes Morgan's solution to the problem of changing a primitive, recalcitrant kingdom into "the Republic" (389).

Twain could not subscribe to the devout Cable's "Religion" as a progressive force; rather, the Church becomes the greatest opponent to Morgan's "Progress." But "Education" becomes indispensable to the Boss's project: "Training is everything; training is all" (161). Counterpoint to the "mere animal training" of Camelot's white Indians, "teaching-factories" lay the foundations for a great cultural revolution with profound political implications, "the first of its kind in the history of the world—a rounded and complete governmental revolution without bloodshed" (366). Seeking to end the caste system by demonstrating its industrial inefficiency and by educating a younger generation of technocrats who have no allegiance to the old ways, Morgan finally achieves what appears to be total victory with the help of two revolvers: "A happy and prosperous country, and strangely altered" (364). Sir Boss even weds a sixth-century women, Sandy, and their domestic bliss, replete with their child Hello-Central, would appear to figure the accommodation of the sixth-century to the Yankee standards of 1879, the year Morgan identifies as his present moment.

But if Morgan, Sandy, and Hello-Central are the picture of the Victorian family, their sixth-century world is less an anticipatory replica of the late nineteenth-century United States than a colonial conquest modernized at gunpoint. Even as a very modern conflict with an iron worker sends Morgan off to a preindustrial age, modernization itself disrupts Morgan's project as bad feelings generated by stock-market losses puts into circulation Sir Lancelot's trysts with Queen Guinevere. The figurative rendition of the South's Redemption, the medieval Church's Interdict against Sir Boss's model of progress, returns England to the bad old days of slavery and arbitrary aristocratic rule. But unlike the Compromise of 1877 that resulted in the withdrawal of federal troops from the South and left redeemed Southern states to implement Jim Crow, Morgan and his young, educated adherents vow to stay and fight until the bitter end.

The horrific Battle of the Sand-Belt that ends *A Connecticut Yankee* dispels any possibility of reconciliation between the rebellious slave master knights and the progressive reformers. Sir Boss, Clarence, and the fifty-two teenagers prevail over 25,000 knights, but their great victory is also their defeat. The very industrial efficiency of their defensive emplacements becomes what Clarence describes as "a trap of our own making"; the immense scale of the slaughter guarantees the reformers' death by old-fashioned pestilence (406). Unhappily separated from Sandy and Hello-Central by the unbridgeable gulf of modernity, Morgan can only mourn the failed Reconstruction and his now-impossible family life. *A Connecticut Yankee* undercuts the very possibility of imagining nation building through marriage as even Morgan's domestic life is less the result of a modern consensual romance than the formalizing of a white Indian custom: "I had married her for no particular reason, except that by the customs of chivalry she was my property until some knight should win her from me in the field" (372).

The point here is not to rehearse the historical debate over whether the victorious North should consider the defeated South as a conquered territory subject to imperial military rule or as states that merely required the formal abolition of slavery to reenter the Union. Rather, the imperial framework that informs both models of nation building required the subordination of all those racialized as nonwhite: Indians (white or otherwise) or the freedmen. In *A Connecticut Yankee*, a civil war destroys Camelot, but one wonders if Morgan might have well succeeded had he launched his planned imperial conquest of the Western Hemisphere; just before the Interdict, Sir Boss "was getting ready to send out an expedition to discover America" (365). If the events of the 1880s—white mob violence in the form of lynching and rapes, the systematic disenfranchisement of the black vote, the overturning of federal civil rights legislation in the courts—lead Twain to a radically different conclusion about the possibility of national reunion than Cable, then their romances of reunion, successful or not, depended upon the racial figurations of U.S. imperial nation building. Whether overcoming white Indians or being overcome by them, these texts highlight the anxious imperial imaginings at the root of post-Reconstruction national allegory and the implied perils of a renewed U.S. imperialism.

National Texts, Imperial Contexts

The chapters that follow trace the displacement of the problematic narrative of North and South with the imperialist East-West configuration of national identity. While each narrative examined is unique in its articulation of the representational crisis in national identity, taken together these texts suggest the centrality of a renewed imperialist narrative that would propel the United States into the twentieth century as a formidable colonial and neocolonial power. Their authors—the highly canonical Henry James, the semi-canonical Helen Hunt Jackson, and the recently recovered María Amparo Ruiz de Burton—wrote historical romances during the 1880s in which the imperial dynamics of national allegory figure prominently. This grouping—an expatriate aesthete, a passionate New England reformer, and a dispossessed Californiana—covers a wide range of U.S. writers who grappled with the imperial formation of national identity, but from very different social positions and with very different concerns. Starting with James's *The Bostonians*, the study proceeds to the imperial East-West displacement of North and South by the unfinished colonial project out West in Jackson's *Ramona* and in Ruiz de Burton's *The Squatter and the Don*. Situated at the critical vantage point of the mid-1880s, these novels responded to the increasingly technological and scientific locus of imperialist thought suggested by the slightly later *A Connecticut Yankee*.

Ever aware of the United States's own colonial history, James self-consciously cast *The Bostonians* as a romance of reunion in his desire to write "a very *American* novel" (*Complete Notebooks* 47). This novel indicates most acutely the ideological crisis of national allegory in imagining a North-South national consensus. Representational failures structure *The Bostonians*, starting with James's claim not to be able to depict Basil Ransom's Mississippian accent on the printed page. The widespread use of dialect in U.S. realist fiction of the day represented for James the dangerous dynamics of a global imperialist project that, far from ensuring the dominance of Anglo-Saxon civilization, ultimately threatened the very binary oppositions of colonizer and colonized upon which it was based.

Feminist encroachments into the public sphere, at first confined to the radical feminist Bostonians of the novel but becoming a general disposition of U.S. women some twenty years later in *The American Scene*, signaled for James the ultimate undermining of a coherent, legible U.S. national identity. The failed romance of reunion in *The Bostonians* uneasily acknowledges the imperial origins of the cultural privileges of whiteness on one hand and on the other bemoaned the very modernity that U.S. imperialism brought into existence. The deferred, unhappy wedding of Southerner Basil Ransom and the working-class Yankee Verena Tarrant, and the imagined reunion of North and South, ultimately indicates the crisis in U.S. national identity created by U.S. imperialism, implied by dialect, and promoted by white women. In effect, national (re)union could no longer be narrated at all.

Displacing the North-South problem with the nation-building consolidation of imperial conquests out West, Jackson's 1884 historical romance *Ramona* attempted to stir public opinion in the name of a nascent Indian reform movement. Seeking to atone for the nation's bloody "Century of Dishonor" in its duplicitous dealings with tribal nations, Jackson hoped to transmute the unindividuated savage of the tribe into a person before federal law, and ultimately, into a citizen. Drawing upon recently developed anthropological theories of civilizational development, Jackson depicts colonized Native Americans of Southern California as having already internalized the Victorian ideals of Christianity, private property, domesticity, and wage labor through the racial tutelage of the Roman Catholic missions and the Californio *ranchos*. Even as the novel deplores white racist violence against assimilated Indian families, it participates in the imperialist genocide of tribal nations as well; the very structure of racial tutelage that allows for the civilization of savages also ensures that project would always remain radically incomplete. Ultimately, the racialized nation-building logic of Jackson's historical romance erases alternative modes of social and economic collectivity to legitimate an imperialist U.S. national identity.

Ruiz de Burton's 1885 novel *The Squatter and the Don* marks the imperialist limits of U.S. national allegory. Unlike the other historical romances discussed in this study, the multiple marriages between Californios and patrician white settlers succeed in reproducing families. Seeking to integrate national elites, these marriages secure the whiteness of economically decimated Californio ranchero families by gaining access to entrepreneurial opportunities and liquid financial assets. However, even as the Alamar family ultimately escapes the racialized proletarianization that most Californios were experiencing by the 1870s as a result of their racialized status, another force threatens to undo their national incorporation as white citizens. The Southern Pacific Railroad looms ominously as an alternative imperialist collectivity that could invert U.S. racial hierarchies by enslaving whites. Blocking the invisible hand of the market, the "black" transnational monopoly in effect mirrored the "black misrule" of Reconstruction by destroying the privileges of whiteness. Ultimately, the economic might of the imperial transnational corporation rewrites the national narrative of freedom as one as enslavement, casting the very possibility of national allegory into doubt. Writing in the aftermath of Manifest Destiny's imperial run over the continent, Ruiz de Burton anticipates the new technologically based U.S. imperialist imaginary of the coming American Century.

As an epilogue, I examine some implications of reinterpreting the national parameters of literary interpretation by rereading *Ramona* through Cuban expatriate José Martí's 1891 translation of that novel into Spanish. Transforming what Jackson considered to be a national problem of Indian incorporation into a meditation upon the hemispheric conundrum of race, Martí subtly rewrote Jackson's racial liberalism into a potential strategy for true racial and cultural equality across the Americas. By doing so, Martí suggests how national allegories, and nationalist interpretive strategies, must be jettisoned to fight the impending expansion of the U.S. empire built upon the invidious difference between a global North and a global South.

CHAPTER 2

Speaking American

Henry James
and the
Dialect of Modernity

Writing a series of commentaries titled "American Letters" for the British periodical *Literature* at the height of the Spanish-American War, Henry James complained in "The American Novel of Dialect" that "[n]othing is more striking, in fact, than the invasive part played by the element of dialect in the subject-matter of the American fiction of the day" (699). Even as an overseas American Empire was coming to fruition, James fretfully addressed the question cultural difference might have upon national culture. Commenting that Edward Townsend's 1895 novel *Chimmie Fadden* consisted of the "very riot of the abnormal—the dialect of the New York newsboy and bootblack," James bemoaned the extent to which the aesthetics of fiction had been reduced to the mere "cleverness" of a mimetic transcription of "'modernity,' of contemporary newspaperese" (700; 698). Much to James's dismay, undiscriminating readers encouraged this trend by voraciously consuming novels of dialect. While novels of dialect might be bestsellers, James continued, these "great successes are not the studies of the human plant under cultivation" (700). Rather than reproducing the proper language through which U.S. letters would accurately reflect a refined national civilization, popular novels perpetuated dialect and thus authorized questionable differences of class, race, and gender in the American republic.

As the United States approached the twentieth century, James's sentiment that the aesthetic standards of national culture were being undermined by the dynamics of the mass reading market reflects his anxieties about the tenuous sense of national inheritance. Upon its surface, James's diatribe against a philistine mass culture in the "The American Novel of Dialect" has the familiar ring of Jamesian insistence upon the complete autonomy of high cultural aesthetics. Yet at the very moment of U.S. imperial expansion that heralded the dawn of the American Century, James's comments about dialect are not so much disconnected from the political, economic, and racial dynamics of that imperialism but rather an anxious claim to aesthetic autonomy in the name of the never completed project of Anglo-American cultural renewal. James's splenetic comments about the novel of dialect reflect not just his preoccupation with the United States's lack of cultural resources vis-à-vis "Europe" but also the uneasy consequences of imperialist nation building for the sense of U.S. nationhood itself. James's cultural project of national renewal through the novel inhabits (even as it reinvents) the transnational racial category of Anglo-American civilization, following the imperial logic by which national borders might fluctuate but correspondingly through which whiteness as a marker of colonial difference could be continuously remade.[1]

Usually situated in a cosmopolitan, transatlantic context, James has seldom been considered a theorist, or even proponent, of U.S. nationalism and its imperialist practices. Much more common has been the critical sense of James as being, if anything, "anti-American" in his geographic and aesthetic positioning after his 1875 transatlantic migration to Europe. Writing upon the occasion of James's death, T. S. Eliot suggested that James's commitment to the very principle of the nation, much less to the particular nation called the United States, stood on precarious ground: "It is the final perfection, the consummation of an American to become not an Englishman, but a European, something which no born European, no person of any European nationality can become" (855). James's brother William would similarly place him outside the realm of nationality altogether, remarking, "He's really, I won't say a Yankee, but a native of the James family, and has no other country" (qtd. in Matthiessen 303).

However, the critical emphasis upon James as a Europeanized expatriate has obscured his deep engagement, aesthetic and otherwise, with U.S. social relations. If literary scholars have traditionally interpreted Jamesian formal complexity as solely aesthetic and not as the socially embedded figurations of Lionel Trilling's more relational "restless analyst," then neither view takes James's seeming indifference to portrayals of "race" or to the context of late nineteenth-century imperialism as anything other than that.[2] Consequently, that Toni Morrison should name "Henry James scholarship" as the prime example of the "willed scholarly indifference" to the ghostly literary presence of the U.S. imperial project seems only appropriate (13). Heeding Morrison's call to excavate the Jamesian entanglement with the cultures of U.S. imperialism, more recent scholarship by Sara Blair, Walter Benn Michaels, Ross Posnock, and Kenneth Warren have shown how James's literary aesthetics variously negotiated the social complexities of the late nineteenth-century world.

Far from positing a sphere of pure art, Jamesian realism participated within contested ideological transformations of imperial racial formations; in Warren's words, "racial concerns shaped James's aesthetic even when his texts were not specifically 'about' race in any substantive way" (12).[3] Insofar as "race" and "culture" were inextricably linked in the logic of imperialism during the Age of Empire, the proper reproduction of the latter inevitably invoked anxieties about the reproduction of the former. As Jonathan Freedman has noted on James's relation to U.S. nationalism, "The translation of empire . . . is one with the transmission of culture," particularly for a nation that "had in his youth been rent asunder in the Civil War and was struggling in his middle years to reconstruct itself on a new, imperial model" (7–8). This becomes most apparent in James's commentary on dialect in U.S. novels at the moment of the U.S.-Spanish War, where James explicitly argued for the racial implications of that specific realist narrative strategy for the making of a U.S. national civilization. A reconsideration of dialect's functioning within Jamesian aesthetics results in a significantly revised understanding of the relationship James posits between realism, imperialism, and national identity.

At odds with conservative white supremacist writers such as Joel Chandler Harris and Thomas Nelson Page as well as liberal advocates of black civil rights such as Mark Twain and George Washington Cable, James repudiated the increasingly popular use of dialect in the nation's metropolitan magazines such as *Century Magazine, Atlantic Monthly, Harper's Weekly,* and the *North American Review* during the 1880s. When *The Bostonians* began its thirteen-month serial run in the February 1885 issue of *Century Magazine,* the narrative shared the pages with Joel Chandler Harris's renditions of antebellum plantation songs as well as selections from Twain's just-published subscription novel, *The Adventures of Huckleberry Finn.* While far from being assured the importance in U.S. literary history that Ernest Hemingway would later assign to it, *Huckleberry Finn* garnered praise not only for its dialect in conversations between its characters, but also for its adoption of dialect for the point of view. Although the trustees of the Concord (New Hampshire) Public Library banned the novel in March 1885 on the grounds that "it is couched in the language of a rough, ignorant dialect," most reviewers praised its use of dialect as, in the words of plantation dialect writer Harris, "the most original contribution that has yet been made to American literature" (qtd. in Fischer 16; Harris 4).

As Michael North has noted, the black dialect employed by white writers such as Harris helped construct the post-Reconstruction myth of harmonious race relations between planters and slaves, a useful construct with which to demonize the freedmen and to legitimate Jim Crow and white supremacy. So despite the implied racial egalitarianism of Twain's narrative, even staunch white Southern ideologues such as Harris embraced the liberal use of dialect within *Huckleberry Finn*. Responding in an *Atlanta Constitution* editorial to the library ban, Harris defended *Huckleberry Finn*, calling it "an almost artistically perfect picture of life and character in the southwest . . . equally valuable to the historian and to the student of sociology" (4). In appealing to sociological and historical grounds as well as aesthetic ones for the use of dialect (including his own), Harris invoked the authority of newly professionalized disciplines that self-consciously involved themselves in excavating a racialized genealogy of national civilization.[4] The use of American dialects distinguished U.S. writing from other national traditions; by transcending the manifestly political content of any text, dialect in effect became the literary sign of the United States itself.

James's response to dialect, "The American Novel of Dialect," situates the development of a high cultural aesthetic in apparent opposition to the uncertain effects of imperial nation building, the results of which included culturally marginal populations and the mass culture that catered to them. For James, the U.S. novel of dialect challenged the very possibility of aesthetic production, begging "the question of the possible bearing, on the art of the representation of manners, of the predominance more and more enjoyed by the representation of those particular manners with which dialect is intimately allied." In carelessly participating within the economic dictates of mass culture, U.S. novelists had allowed the representational strategy of dialect to determine the social horizons of the realist novel. Dialect had in effect colonized the realist novel, forcing fiction to devolve into squalid depictions of working-class life in which "colloquial speech arrives at complete debasement" (699). In what he saw as the narrowing of fiction's social field, James found novels of dialect "curiously suggestive of how little the cultivation of the truth of vulgar linguistics is a guarantee of the cultivation of any other truth" (698).

The "truth" of dialect for James lay rather in the very fact of its widespread use as a realist narrative strategy. He attributed the quest "for dialectical treasure" to the specific circumstances of an expansive and expanding white race for empire: "[The novel of dialect] is a part, in its way, to all appearance, of the great general wave of curiosity on the subject of the soul aboundingly *not* civilized that has lately begun to roll over the Anglo-Saxon globe" (698–99). For James, novels of dialect represented a kind of uncanny reverse colonization of the senses occurring within the heart of the empire that threatened the renewal of Anglo-Saxon civilization. Whether representing the speech of racialized colonial subjects abroad or unruly wage laborers at home, dialect not only represented those who had been largely excluded from the domain of proper fiction but also disseminated the very circumstances of being uncivilized.

The danger, then, for James lay in that these representations of "uncultivated" speech threatened to erode the crucial differences between colonizer and colonized, workers and "their betters," by displacing the aesthetic practice of studying "the human plant under cultivation" with broken English renditions of "extreme barbarism" (699–700). Only the pitch and tone of civilization stood as the guarantee of civilized difference from the colonized abroad and the "dangerous classes" at home. Couching his terms in the Arnoldian dichotomy of culture and anarchy now globally projected, James argued that national degradation was the inevitable trajectory of U.S. letters in the absence of countervailing narratives of "civilization." The danger loomed largest for the young United States, just then entering the overseas scramble for empire. In contrast, older imperial European nations had preserved "a tradition of portrayal . . . of those who are the product of circumstances more complex" (699). Despite their imperial entanglements, the field of representation had not been abdicated completely to the "rigorously hard conditions" of the colonized or the urban underclass. Great Britain may have its share of Rudyard Kiplings, but that nation also had the refined Mary Augusta Ward. Among the French, Paul Bourget's novels counterbalanced the works of a "handful of close observers of special rustic manners" (700).

In contrast to the numerous writers of dialect, James felt that the United States had only William Dean Howells, who, while a fine writer, best addressed "the democratic passion" that admitted little sense of "cultivation" (700). James's concern, then, was that national distinction would come under erasure by the imperial need to represent how the other half lived. The imperial imperative to colonize involved producing the necessary discursive knowledge of those who once could simply be excluded from national literary representations. Imperial aesthetics could mobilize dialect as one strategy of constructing colonial difference as a specific cultural practice, and thus as an object of an ethnographic, imperial knowledge, but at the same time risked erasing the very differences of civilization it sought to establish by incorporating representations of savage natives or a surly working class within the refined national consciousness.

Making the utterings and corresponding social conditions of an increasingly racialized post-Reconstruction urban working class emblematic of the nation, the U.S. novel of dialect threatened to redefine the letters of the Yankee republic as a challenge to, rather than an example of, the very idea of a legible, coherent national civilization. James feared the shelling of Boston by a belligerent Spanish fleet at the time he wrote "The American Novel of Dialect" in July 1898, but the linguistic challenge posed by working-class immigrants and other marginalized subjects eventually became a more fundamental threat to the older Yankee imagined community of his youth. Foreign accents might well achieve what foreign fleets could not.

Stowe, Du Bois, and Nationalist Aesthetics

If the new U.S. imperialism had brought about the turn-of-the-century rush for "dialectical treasures," then the world stage of mass culture had been prepared by the even older dynamics of a previous U.S. imperialism rooted in slavery. James traced the turn-of-the-century literary fascination with dialect, and consequently realist representations of gender, race, and class, to the domestic fictions of Harriet Beecher Stowe. As the "American novel that has made most noise in the world," *Uncle Tom's Cabin* marked for James the historical moment at which U.S. narrative became rooted in "rigorously hard conditions and a fashion of English—or call it of American—more or less abnormal" ("American Novel of Dialect" 700). As Kenneth Warren has noted, Stowe is the signal presence within James's 1886 novel *The Bostonians* of disruptive feminist interventions within the national public sphere. Basil Ransom's pointed reference to James's fictional rendition of Stowe, the abolitionist author Eliza P. Moseley, "as the cause of the biggest war of which history preserves the record," paraphrases Abraham Lincoln's more benign reference to Stowe as "the little lady who made this big war" (qtd. in Warren 94).

Ransom's rhetorical question—"The Abolitionists brought [the Civil

War] on, and were not the Abolitionists principally females?"—suggests that the nation-tearing trauma found its roots within women's transgression of the boundaries between the public and domestic spheres (84). Just as female abolitionists of the 1850s justified their public actions by the moral imperative to end slavery, the feminist movement of *The Bostonians* invoked the slave-like status of white women themselves as the rationale for their public speeches.[5] This entanglement of gender and race as sites of male, imperial oppression became for James the troubling knot that tied aesthetics and politics, the white middle-class domestic sphere with black slave spirituals, Stowe at the middle of the nineteenth century and W. E. B. Du Bois at the beginning of the next.

Judging from his comments about Stowe and Du Bois, James could have scarcely entertained the current inclusion of these authors within the U.S. literary canon. To the extent that both Stowe and Du Bois focused upon gender and racial domination, James suggests that they and their works could not be considered truly "national" in scope. In his 1913 autobiography, *A Small Boy and Others*, James dismissed *Uncle Tom's Cabin* as an evocative, "wonderful 'leaping' fish" that had circumvented the literary realm altogether, "much less a book than a state of vision, of feeling and of consciousness." Stowe's domestic novel was no novel at all, insofar as readers did not critically "read and appraise" but only "walked and talked and laughed and cried." This mass cultural phenomenon circumvented "conscious criticism" altogether, thus affirming for James that "appreciation and judgment, the whole impression, were thus an effect for which there had been no [critical] process." In lieu of a self-reflexive critical response, *Uncle Tom's Cabin* and its stage productions instead generated an anti-nationalist political reaction. Relying upon unexamined sentiment rather than critical aesthetic distinctions, Stowe's novel made but one distinction among its audience—"Northern as differing from Southern"— with nation-tearing implications (*A Small Boy* 92). Categorically splitting the nation into abolitionist or slaveholder, Stowe's "flying fish" of a narrative had inappropriately amalgamated fish and fowl, domestic hearth and public stage, literary aesthetics and political polemics. *Uncle Tom's Cabin* could only divide the Union with its radical critique of the pre–Civil War national consensus.

The half century separating Stowe's novel and Du Bois's *The Souls of Black Folk* brought new modes of racial domination, yet James's assessment of the racial politics of narration and nation did not seem to register the difference. After Harvard University professor William James encouraged his brother to read the work of Du Bois, a former student of his at Harvard, the younger James implied that *The Souls of Black Folk*, being "the only 'Southern' book of any distinction published for many a year," was merely provincial and not national (*The American Scene* 697). James defined "Southern" as the sectional "monomania" of slavery's apologists during the quarter-century preceding the Civil War, as well as its ghostly afterlife (698). James's conflation of the Northern-reared and Harvard-educated Du Bois ("that most accomplished of members of the negro race") with the South as a region and slavery as a context casts the early twentieth-century issues of racial domination and civil rights as part of a superannuated sectional past (697).

For James, the post-Reconstruction shift from slavery to segregation was merely a peculiar regional characteristic that did not touch upon the nation's modern identity. In his acerbic 1907 travel narrative *The American Scene*, the South itself seemed to him "a sort of sick lioness who has so visibly parted with her teeth and claws that we may patronizingly walk all around her" (697). To trade real aesthetic concerns for fatuous political purposes meant crossing the dividing line between the appropriately critical knowledge of aesthetic practice and the improperly divisive knowledge of racial and gender politics. For James, Stowe and Du Bois apparently had crossed that line, subordinating the creation of a properly national culture to the exigencies of a transient political moment. In disavowing the national relevance of Stowe and Du Bois, James considered the civil rights struggles of white women and African Americans as too partial, provincial, and aesthetically inappropriate for U.S. literature. Insofar as he imagined the white supremacist ordering of Jim Crow and lynching to be Southern and emphatically not national, James dismissed the possibility that racialized regimes of violence and exclusion would fundamentally underwrite U.S. national identity itself by the turn of the century.

Yet James's explicit articulation of discourses of gender, race, and nation, along with the less visible but no less important class dimensions, highlights the necessity of resituating James as a post-Reconstruction intellectual who theorized the layered boundaries of national inclusion and exclusion. The fate of national civilization in the age of mass culture, particularly a national literature's function and place within modernity, preoccupied James throughout his professional career but emerged most acutely in the texts that foreground the question of national identity. "The American Novel of Dialect" appears roughly midway in the twenty-year gap between two Jamesian texts that closely interrogate nation building during the post-Reconstruction period: *The Bostonians* and *The American Scene*. From his explicit refusal to write in dialect in *The Bostonians* to his condemnations of the "Accent of the Future" in *The American Scene* and other essays written after his 1904–5 return visit to the United States, James articulated a specifically literary agenda of racial-cultural renewal designed to shore up the nation against the cultural challenges posed by women, African Americans, and immigrants.

If the national patrimony represented by the English language had been put at risk by novels of dialect, then properly literary novels could potentially provide an aesthetic haven from the pressure of vulgar language usage on the streets. As Sara Blair has demonstrated, James's concern over the state of fiction writing in the mid-1880s stemmed from his desire to foster "the cultivation of the English novel as an instrument of the higher critical and moral intelligence of the race" (83). Yet even as James employed the novel of cultivation in order to renew national culture, *The Bostonians* represents the historical limits of the novel for rescuing a national culture. Subject to, and in fact part of, the very modernity that it was meant to redress, the novel form exhibited the social stresses ventriloquized in dialect by precisely those subordinated, colonized populations who contested the consensus narrative of U.S. history in the Age of Empire. Over the course of the post-Reconstruction era, James's agonistic engagement with dialect necessarily exposed the profound racial, gender, and class violence at the heart of the imperial nation's writ.

The Bostonians: "A Very American Tale"

Coming off the critical and commercial successes of *Daisy Miller*, *The Europeans*, and *The Portrait of a Lady*, James wrote in his journal entry of April 8, 1883, that he was embarking upon "an attempt to show that I *can* write an American story" (*Complete Notebooks* 19). Anxious to demonstrate that his European migration had not in any way diminished his American experience, James wanted "the whole thing as local, as American, as possible" (19). Despite his best efforts to write "a very *American* tale, a tale characteristic of our social condition, and life," James found *The Bostonians* to be his most dismal failure of novelistic representation (47). The "unhappy" novel, first serialized in *Century Magazine* beginning in February 1885 and later published in its entirety in 1886, seemed "born under an evil star" (31). Initially planning to write six installments, James found he could not finish the narrative in under thirteen, all the while under pressure to deliver *The Princess Cassimassima* for the *Atlantic Monthly*. The first installment caused a controversy over what many believed to be James's satirical portrait of Nathaniel Hawthorne's sister-in-law Elizabeth Peabody in the character of Miss Birdseye. In particular, he found his brother William's criticism on this point "a very cold douche indeed" (*Letters* 3:70).

But even this controversy could not conjure a reading public for *The Bostonians*. James would later recall that Richard Gilder, editor of *Century Magazine*, wrote to him that "they had never published anything that appeared so little to interest their readers" (*Letters* 4:778). Financially, the novel proved equally disastrous. The Boston publishing firm of James R. Osgood, which had serialization and publication rights for the United States and Great Britain, went bankrupt in May 1885, leaving the novel's publication in suspension until James could recover the publication rights and renegotiate a contract with the British firm of Macmillan & Co. The novel sold poorly even then, and failed to garner much critical interest. James wrote dejectedly to his brother, "I hoped much of it, and shall be disappointed—having got no money for it, I hoped for a little glory" (*Letters* 3:89). Diagnosing the novel's critical and financial failure as a disturbing slippage of narrative mastery, James would write to William that "[a]ll the middle part is too diffuse and insistent—far too describing and explaining and expatiating. The whole thing is too long and dawdling. This come from the fact (partly) that I had the sense of knowing terribly little about the kind of life I had attempted to describe—and felt a constant pressure to make the picture substantial by thinking it out—penciling and 'shading'" (*Letters* 3:91). The subsequent exclusion of *The Bostonians* (along with *Washington Square*) from the New York edition further marginalized the novel from James's already fading popularity. Late in life, James wrote of his desire to revise the narrative and write a critical preface for a new edition but acknowledged that "there can be no question of that . . . at present, or probably ever within the span of my life" (*Letters* 4:778).

Usually situating *The Bostonians* within James's realist middle period, contemporary critics have noted the anomalous position it occupies within both the Jamesian canon and the post–Civil War novelistic genre of the "romance of reunion." In defiance of generic conventions, James makes the Southerner of the romantic pairing not a woman but the hyper-masculine Basil Ransom, while the Northerner is the working-class, socially marginal Verena Tarrant rather than the more typical Yankee soldier or businessman. Despite this deviation from "the standard formula for reconciliation," Nina Silber reads *The Bostonians* as a confirmation of a conservative social ordering of gender relations that James sets against the Gilded Age's "damnable feminization" as manifested in the growing influence of women in public life (118). Silber's characterization of James's opinions may be largely correct, but in a certain way *The Bostonians* is less a confirmation of nationalized gender hierarchies than an uncertain deployment of such gender relations for nationalizing projects.[6] Problematizing the romance of reunion altogether, *The Bostonians* highlights the difficulties posed by the feminist movement's articulation of racial and gender oppression for post-Reconstruction nation building, an articulation that had been made at least a half-century earlier during the coalescing of the abolitionist movement.

"The Emancipation of Our Sex"

At one point in *The Bostonians*, feminist orator Verena Tarrant banters with erstwhile suitor Basil Ransom, proposing that he join her on a national speaking circuit so they could "go round together as poison and antidote." Refusing to sanction the appearance of any woman in the public eye, much less publicly debate the feminist characterization of history as the rank oppression of women by men, Ransom declines to enter the spectacular war between the sexes. The conservative ex-slaveholder responds with a suggestion of his own: "I think I should be able to interpret history for you in a new light" (85). In privately contesting what he considers to be the bad revisionist history of the feminist movement circa 1880, Ransom believes he can restore the properly man-made historical course of national, sexual, and racial relations that the feminist movement frequently contested during and after Reconstruction.

Undaunted, Verena later tells the staunchly anti-feminist Ransom that women's liberation "is only a question of time—the future is ours." But despite her proleptic optimism, Verena also admits that the present situation for women in the struggle against patriarchy is not so rosy: "Everywhere we heard one cry—'How long, Lord, how long?'" (210). Appropriating the world-weary cry for freedom uttered by enslaved African Americans, Verena identifies the plight of women with that of slaves before Emancipation. Turning on its head the maxim of nineteenth-century colonial ethnography that the status of women reflected the level of national and cultural progress, the feminist movement, closely identified in *The Bostonians* with Verena and her wealthy friend Olive Chancellor, cast the status of white women as that of slaves not yet freed.[7] Rewriting Victorian domesticity as the latest chapter in the history of human bondage, Verena and Olive threaten to declare what historian Catherine Clinton calls "The Other Civil War," or the nineteenth-century struggle for women's rights.[8] Excoriating the likes of the ex-Confederate Ransom, unreformed representative of patriarchal men "who, no doubt, desired to treat women with the lash and manacles, as he and his people had formerly treated the wretched coloured race," the feminist movement in *The Bostonians* challenged the consensus history of national civilization (150).

The abolitionist project of dividing the Union over the "peculiar institution" appeared to be only the first step towards an even more radical post-Reconstruction feminist goal: emancipating women from the domestic sphere altogether. Reconstruction-era feminists had often deployed abolitionist language to describe their own condition in an attempt to mobilize public support for voting rights. During the heated debates over the proposed Fifteenth Amendment in 1869, abolitionist-feminist Pauline Wright Davis, urging passage of a version that would have extended suffrage to both African Americans and women, asked, "When will women realize that they are slaves, and with one mind and one heart, strike the blow which will set them free?" (qtd. in E. C. Du Bois 74).

For Olive, realizing women's enslaved status is cast as always remembering women's oppression at the hands of men, "the brutal, bloodstained, ravening race" (34–35). Ever having "the image of the unhappiness of women" before her, Olive visualizes how "ages of oppression had rolled over them" and "uncounted millions had lived only to be tortured, to be crucified" (34). The result of remembering past oppression, according to James, is that white women ceased to think of themselves as "Americans" and started to consider themselves as enslaved foreigners, a term the narrative identifies with the freedmen. "What else were the Africans?" the narrative asks rhetorically, but "foreigners?" (26). Patriarchy makes men and women foreigners to each other, such that Olive fears that Verena will marry "an enemy of her country" of women (150). Collectively imagining themselves outside the nation, the feminist movement abjures the need to reproduce the nation through adherence to the dominant gendered division of labor. Ignoring the distinctions that marked the public sphere from the domestic one, and consequently the appropriate behavior for cultured women in each, politically vocal women such as Olive and Verena threatened to undermine the basis of a distinguished and distinguishable U.S. culture through their radical activism.

The danger to the nation that the feminists presented, then, lay not simply in the symptomatic abridgement of the "spheres." Rather, the feminist critique identified the causal connection between those abridgements and the gendered oppression as the very basis of national consensus, a characterization the narrative works to contain even as it rehearses the coercive nature of the seemingly naturalized consensus of marriage. As the novel's final scene implies, the romance of national reunion stages the primal scene of male coercion. Lynn Wardley argues that the logic of gendered violence in *The Bostonians* structures the terms of national reunion; by relegating the naturally theatrical Verena to the domestic sphere of familial and cultural reproduction, Ransom naturalizes the marital union that guarantees the necessary precondition of the male citizen's individuality in mass democracy. The spectacular assassination of the feminist movement, along with other political acts of violence, forges the nation: "Assassination, then, like civil war—and, we would add, like the sacrifice of women to private life so that 'every man' can 'keep himself aloof'—is absorbed into democracy's body" in order to enable the nation's existence (Wardley 661).

Waxing violent, Ransom feels "capable of kidnapping" Verena from Boston's Music Hall stage and practically does so "by muscular force" (364; 418). Verena's protestations are muffled when Ransom "thrust the hood of Verena's long cloak over her head," thus removing not only the possibility of her public address but also her public identity as a feminist. But Verena's transformation into a *femme covert* through marriage does not so much restore what Ransom believes to be the natural order of the patriarchal family and nation but rather points to the dramatic failure of such imaginings. The famously problematic last sentence of *The Bostonians* thus indicates a crisis of narrative closure not entirely within the Master's control: "It is to be feared that with the union, so far from brilliant, into which she was about to enter, these [tears] were not the last she was destined to shed" (418). Rather than celebrate the allegorical reunion of North and South through the wedding of Verena and Ransom, the ultimate words of the narrative cast doubt upon the affective security of their, and the nation's, union. The narrative defers the wedding itself even as it lends portents of future trials for the married couple. For James's post-Reconstruction national allegory, then, marriage may be necessary, but not necessarily consensual.

Yet this aesthetic failure to enact a consensual romance of reunion is less a feminist critique of a coercive patriarchal order than a trace of a larger aesthetic problem of realist representation. Even if Ransom ultimately succeeds in stopping up Verena's mouth with marital kisses, his own pronouncements come under the erasure of James's realist aesthetics. James disavows Ransom's Mississippian accent at the onset of the novel, claiming that it was literally unrepresentable on the printed page: "It is not within my power to reproduce by any combination of characters this charming dialect" (4). While James may cagily cast his rejection of dialect as an intentional failure of authorial mastery, Ransom's provincial, heterogeneous pronunciation proves to be a problem of realist literary depiction that James can neither fully represent nor completely deny, but can only foreground as a question of national aesthetics. These two queerly un-Jamesian suspensions of narrative mastery in *The Bostonians*, one cannily self-proclaimed and the other only uncannily implied, emerge symptomatically as James's anxieties about the racial and cultural purity of the nation and the strained possibilities of its renewal under the perniciously transformative conditions of modernity.

While Olive, Verena, and the other feminists of the novel most clearly figure James's fears of national disunity, Ransom himself represents the white belligerent masculinity required not only for enforcing the ostensibly consensual romance of reunion, but also the racialist dangers of just such an nation-building endeavor. Even if James demurred to write in dialect, Ransom's voice still carries within it the long legacy of cultural hybridity, both pre- and post-Emancipation, which haunts James's description: Ransom's "discourse was pervaded by something sultry and vast, something almost African in its rich, basking tone, something that suggested the teeming expanse of the cotton-field" (4). The Mississippian accent embodies the violence of slavery that made Ransom "rich" and "basking" at the expense of the black slaves working in the whiteness of the cotton fields. Embedded within Ransom's voice, then, are the figurations of the pre-Emancipation Southern plantation society and the corresponding linguistic miscegenation that James heard, but could not represent, in Ransom's voice. James's decision to forego the use of dialect reflects what Ernest Renan, in his 1882 lecture at the Sorbonne, called the nationalist necessity of being (in Benedict Anderson's translation) "obliged already to have forgotten" the violent circumstances of the establishment of the new nation's writ (qtd. in *Imagined Communities* 200). Remembering projects of national liberation less as the achievement of freedom than as continued racial enslavement, Ransom's accent reveals something even more perilous to the post-Reconstruction whiteness: an always-already misceginated U.S. nationality that speaks with a hybrid tongue. Unable to meet the racially pristine requirements of a national civilization forged in the forgetting of imperial violence, *The Bostonians* can only symptomatically display the traces of this violence in its uncertain, incomplete enactment of marital and national unions.

The Bostonians figures what James would come to see as an even greater threat to U.S. nationhood at the turn of the century. While post-Reconstruction feminism challenged the "romance of reunion" by analogizing the oppression of women with oppression of slaves, the expansionary dynamics of U.S. capital, labor, and empire would even more dramatically undermine the basis of national identity. For James, the immigration to the United States of those clearly marginal to the northern European cultural inheritance—Jews, southern Europeans, and others ambiguously positioned within the imperial ordering of "races"—begged the question of the nation's very existence. With U.S. women taking a cue from their radical Bostonian sisters, the very reproduction of U.S. nationalism seemed in great peril during such drastic changes in demographics. If in the mid-1880s the question of extending the rights of U.S. nationality to two historically subordinated groups—women and the freedmen—came to dominate James's unease at national inclusion, then twenty years later the question for James would become one of the survival of national civilization itself.

The American Scene: Dissolving the Nation

Losing his way through the New Hampshire hills, James described the perplexing experience of asking for directions in *The American Scene*. After an inquiry in English produced only a blank stare, James, noting that his would-be informer "had a dark-eyed 'Latin' look," proceeded to inquire again in French and then Italian. Frustrated with the ensuing silence, he wondered aloud, "What *are* you then?" The immigrant replied, "I'm an Armenian," prompting James to comment in surprise, "As if it were the most natural thing in the world for a wage-earning youth in the heart of New England to be" (455). If the transplanted Armenian considered the encounter mundane, then James the returning "native" did not. In calling attention to the young immigrant's alien status, James claims his nativist rights to a national inheritance. James's surprise lay largely in the realization that not everyone inhabiting the New England landscape necessarily embodied or shared his conception of national belonging.

If James's point in describing the encounter with the Armenian American precludes the narration of its outcome (he does not relate if he received the directions that he needed), and thus only serves to emphasize what he perceived to be the younger man's lack of place within the national fraternity, then the recently arrived immigrant frustrated James's expectation that the English language would interpolate them into a common community where mutual recognition was both natural and national. Rather, James's thwarted attempts at cultural and linguistic categorization highlight the limits of a political imagination based upon a nationalized linguistic tradition. In the face of uncanny faces, James's vision of the United States reveals how the seemingly self-evident intersections of culture and geography made visible the translations of labor and capital across the borders of nationhood. The immigrant, as the unwelcome embodiment of those dynamics, would stand at the margins of national knowledge and cultural citizenship that James would so often ponder in *The American Scene* and other essays about his 1904–5 return visit to the United States.[9]

Shocked and appalled by the vast changes brought about by the massive mobilization of immigrant labor and industrial capital across national borders, James felt the nation's very terms of identity and cohesion to fall under erasure. Feeling "a new chill in his heart," the "restless analyst" writing *The American Scene* found himself doubting the very idea of a coherent national identity. The lived present of "modernity" in the United States—its ever-evolving technologies, its preternaturally fluid urban spaces, its overseas empire, its innumerable immigrants, its feminized consumerism—seemed on the verge of overwhelming the formative processes and institutions that had historically defined what it meant to be an American. Encounters with "alienism unmistakable, alienism undisguised and unashamed," led James to conclude that the previous twenty years had seen the most important relation in life, "one's relation to one's country," undergo a fundamental transformation (459). The international flow of labor and capital had altered the very notion of nation; feeling simultaneously native and alien, James wrote that the very "idea of the country itself underwent something of that profane overhauling through which it appears to suffer the indignity of change" (427).

Nowhere did this appear more vividly apparent for James than at Ellis Island. Visiting "the terrible little" immigrant processing station in the spring of 1905, he watched with fascinated gloom what appeared to him to be the quickening dissolution of national consciousness. Calling the influx of immigrants "an appeal to amazement beyond that of any sword-swallowing or fire-swallowing of the circus," James wondered if this mass spectacle "of ingurgitation on the part of our body politic and social" had not in fact resulted in the phagocytic engulfment of U.S. culture by foreign bodies who not only resisted transformation into "Americans" but also alienated the body politic from its previously native constituents. Far from sharing "the sanctity of his American consciousness, the intimacy of his American patriotism, with the inconceivable alien," the U.S. citizenry found itself reduced to "*unsettled* possession" of a national identity by the immigrant "note of settled possession" (459; emphasis in original).

The immigrant retention of a seemingly foreign cultural identity within the largest U.S. city, New York, only served to emphasize what James saw as the increasing cultural distance not only between his adopted Great Britain and the United States, but also between the Yankee Republic of his youth and the "great commercial democracy" of the turn of the century (432). It seemed that natives had become alienated from the sense of U.S. history as easily as aliens had appropriated the nation. The "modernity" of the United States, James wrote, begged the question of the historical contingency of national identity itself:

> Who and what is an alien, when it comes to that, in a country peopled from the first under the jealous eye of history?—peopled, that is, by migrations at once extremely recent, perfectly traceable and urgently required. . . . Which is the American by these scant measures?—Which is *not* the alien, over a large part of the country at least, and where does one put a finger on the dividing line, or, for that matter, "spot" and identify any particular phase of the conversion, any one of its successive moments? (459)

The antebellum "economic" course of Manifest Destiny, while providing what seemed to be a national history, fundamentally altered the cultural conditions that had brought it into existence. The process by which the jealous eye of Manifest Destiny converted immigrants into Americans also made immigrants of all who were already American. The merely economic circumstances of migration, regardless of the actualities of rooted history or birth, leveled the distinctions between groups who arrived at different historical moments within the narrative of the westward course of empire. In effacing the specific histories of earlier migrations that had established the cultural sense of national feeling, current immigration threatened to make "natives" disappear, just as European colonial immigration had erased the traces of Indians from the land. James feared that, under the conditions of modernity, the United States would soon become the land of the vanishing American.[10]

Indeed, in the closing paragraphs of *The American Scene*, James imagined himself as "a beautiful red man with a tomahawk" dispossessed of the country by the new social order whose rumbling herald was the "missionary Pullman" (735–36). Within James's move of appropriating American indigeneity lies his profound reflection upon the disinheritance of the land's first peoples. Only by inhabiting the racial performance of "redface" could James envision the cultural displacement he felt; he found in his identification with the Indian an imagined subject position that resisted incorporation into the narrative of modernity's progress. However, this figuration is ultimately not so much a symbol of resistance to modernity as merely the superannuated victim of a national developmental narrative.[11]

Finding "no escape from the ubiquitous alien into the future, or even into the present," James attempted to retreat into the past to recover the shreds of national consciousness he found missing from the transformed population (428). But in *The American Scene* the frail sense of the U.S. past, although redolent of personal trial and national reunification, could not stay the destruction of its reminders. Revisiting the Ashburton Place lodgings in Boston where he had, at "the closing-time of the [Civil] War," started his public writing career, James savored this "conscious memento" of the early scene of authorship for the *Nation* some forty years earlier as "the scent lingering in a folded pocket-handkerchief." He revisited Ashburton Place a month later only to find "a gaping void, the brutal effacement, at a stroke, of every related object, of the whole precious past" (543). Upon seeing the absence that was his former home, he commented gloomily, "If I had often seen how fast history could be made I had doubtless never so felt that it could be unmade still faster" (544). James emphasized associative acts of narrative that made for the continuance of personal memory, a sense of place, and national feeling. If bodily senses served to detect the traces of the past left on the landscape, then James's personal past and national history were linked by the bodily act of writing. Erased by the creative destruction of modernity, the scents of history, the scene of writing, and the sense of nation could only fade away. "We've learned the secret of keeping association at bay," James commented (448).

The deafening hum of modernity overwhelmed the tenuous structures of nationalist history, whether inscribed upon the landscape or within personal memory. Nothing characterized this loss of personal and national identity more than the destruction of the homes of his youth. When James discovered that the dwelling where he had been born in the New York City of 1843 had met the same fate as the Ashburton Place house, the "high, square, impersonal structure" that replaced "the ruthlessly suppressed birth-house" on Washington Square could not even serve as a commemoration of James's structure of feeling (431–32). Casting an unwelcome shadow upon the urban landscape, skyscrapers reorganized New York's skyline with a vehemence that appalled James. If the disappearance of his former dwellings disrupted James's connection to the national past, then their replacements prohibited even the idea of history. Rather than read the "tall building" as a sign of social progress through technological advancement, James interpreted skyscrapers as the brutal encroachment of crass commercialism upon the historic U.S. city.[12] Skyscrapers did not, and could not, last long enough to provide the cognitive anchoring of a national landscape.

Even more perniciously, the mere presence of skyscrapers effectively erased the still-existing repositories of U.S. culture. Nowhere was this more apparent for James than in Boston, where the Athenaeum lay prostrate under "the detestable 'tall building' again." James found that the enormous structures surrounding the epitome of an earlier, properly national knowledge defeated any efforts to enter New England's "temple of culture." James lamented, "To approach the Athenaeum [is] only to find all disposition to enter it drop dead as if from quick poison" (546). The curious animation of the philistine edifices illustrated what James saw as an openly hostile anti-historicism of a malignant, commercial agency:

> The brute masses, above the comparatively small refined façade . . . [have] for the inner ear the voice of a pair of school-bullies who hustle and pummel some studious little boy. "'Exquisite' was what they called you, eh? We'll teach you, then, little sneak, to be exquisite! We allow none of that rot round here." (546)

If the bullying skyscrapers with working-class dialects "hustle and pummel" the temple of culture, then their own façades did not provide an alternative nationalist pedagogy for James. Blanketed by windows, the skyscraper's façade spoke "loudest for the economic idea" (435). Windows eliminated the quiet interstices, the dividing lines of public and private that created a cultured environment. The result was an incessant, grating architectural shout that epitomized what the New York conversation, whether of the skyline or the streets, had become.

Precluding a historical narrative of the built environment, the commercialism embodied in skyscrapers had become for James "the local unwritten law that forbids almost any planted object to gather in a history where it stands, forbids in fact any accumulation that may not be recorded in the mere bank-book." Unanchored from all other aspects of the social, history had been reduced to the economic script: "This last became long ago *the* historic page" (474; emphasis in original). Mirroring the constant flux of immigrants upon the streets below in their enforced transience upon the urban scene, the "brute masses" of tall buildings monstrously, corporately doubled the immigrant masses' disruption of the national community, making U.S. culture itself appear at the mercy of the creative destruction of modernity. Linked in their disruption of the national construction of history, the skyscraper and the immigrant, the dual faces of modernity, disrupted the national narration of history with their vulgar voices.

Even the sense of U.S. history itself became subject to this logic of history-destroying commodification. Visiting Washington Irving's house in the Hudson River valley, James deplored that tourists only saw dollar signs where they should instead see the national past. The "'dear' old portraits of the first half of the century" became not indices of the continuity of a nation through history but only commodities within the ever intrusive market, "very dear to-day when properly signed and properly sallow." Writing of Irving's conditions of authorship, James nostalgically cherished the privacy and compactness of U.S. letters during Irving's day, which for him betrayed no sense of the penetration of the market. This "caressing diminutive" vision of authorial autonomy allows James to consider Irving as a nationalist writer whose productions helped inaugurate a cultural sense of what being an "American" meant. In contrast, Irving's house had been transformed into just another tourist site in the eyes of the postnationalist sensibility, which made it impossible to locate authorial production outside the market, or the products of culture to be anything other than commodified nostalgia. Rather, Irving's house and other landmarks of U.S. history had become just another link in the realm of commodities now packaged across the landscape as tourist-trap "places." James lamented, "Modernity, with it pockets full of money and its conscience full of virtue, its heart really full of tenderness, has seated itself there under pretext of guarding the shrine" of national culture (484).

This loss of national history meant nothing less than the loss of national identity for James. The sense of national identity depended upon some perception of a recognizable continuity with the past, or, in other words, a privileged placement within that nation's history. Susan Griffin characterizes the Jamesian narration of the self as one that, in the formulations of functionalist psychology of the turn of the century, composed subjects through the recognition that "without some connection between past and present, identity is lost" (92). Griffin notes James's dilemma over identity in *The American Scene* as a problem of representation generally, and specifically, the problem of representing a nation with so seemingly tenuous a history. According to Griffin, James found the iconographic depiction of history, the strategy of the Hudson River School painters, curiously ahistorical. The illustrations of wildlife and Native Americans in the U.S. landscape increasingly gave the sense of a timeless past while the machines of change entered the garden. For Griffin, the only avenue of historical narrative left to James was the fall into the cycle of imperial fruition and decay, figured as the intrusive consumer-tourist culture inaugurated by the railroad. James's preoccupation with the fate of U.S. national identity, and particularly letters, highlighted concerns over the very possibility of history, whether imagined as the cyclical rise and fall of empire or as the linearly progressive expansion of U.S. democracy. The very possibility of narration itself seemed jeopardized.[13]

The problem of representing the historical continuity of the United States under circumstances that destroyed the very possibilities of such narration plagued James throughout *The American Scene*. In the preface to the New York Edition of *The Portrait of a Lady*, written about the same time as the travelogue, James described how the sense of Italian history, so strongly embodied in the Venetian scenes outside his window, related stories that crowded out his own. "The Venetian footfall and the Venetian cry" frustrated his attempts to fashion narratives other than a properly Italian one. James likened his search for "a lame phrase" for *The Portrait of a Lady* within the Venetian landscape to calling out an "army of glorious veterans" to arrest a vagrant peddler. Its memories organized as the military branch of the nation, Venice spoke in the nationalist accents of historical narrative (1071). *The American Scene* offered no such inspiration; the "Accent of the Future" spoke alarmingly of the blank page the future of U.S. letters promised to become. James concluded, "Certainly, we shall not know it for English—in any sense for which there is an existing literary measure" (470–71). The "Accent of the Future," whether in the novel or on the streets, itself indicated a quickening dissolution of national identity made possible by the experience of what James termed "that profane overhauling" he elsewhere identifies as modernity (427).

If the historic landscape itself became commodified and thus evacuated of national history in *The American Scene*, then James fitfully acknowledged his own complicity with modernity as he sat behind the plate-glass window of the Pullman car as a "restless analyst" whose analysis is enabled by the very conditions of tourist sightseeing he deplored. As Wendy Graham comments, "[m]odernity produces this doubling of consciousness in the subject, who mourns the passing of an older sensibility of intimate personal relation . . . while rapidly habituating himself to the detachment produced by modern conditions" (246). Self-conscious of his modernist dilemma, James distinguished between the fact of modernity and what he believed to be its self-congratulatory hypocrisy about the world it had created. "I accept your ravage," he admitted in an apostrophe to modernity, but what he could not accept was the "pretended message of civilization" that generated "a colossal recipe for the creation of arrears," or the multitude of questions about lack of dense national relations that modernity in the United States left in its wake like "some monstrous unnatural mother might leave a family of unfathered infants on doorsteps or in waiting-rooms" (734–35). At the top of this long list of the arrears was the question of "'American' character" as "the result of such a prodigious amalgam, such a hotch-potch of racial ingredients" (456). If modernity unnaturally propagated the seeming inevitability that white natives faced racial and cultural extinction, then U.S. women would share the blame in not reproducing a properly legitimate nationalist genealogy. The immigrant and the skyscraper, the embodiments of transnational labor and capital, threatened the very possibility of national history itself, while women seemed determined to aid modernity's dissolution of the United States.

Women, Language, and Difference

Immigrant labor and skyscraper-building capital might be destroying a sense of national identity with their respective assaults upon the English language and the very possibility of U.S. history, but this was because Americans, especially women, had traitorously allowed it. In commentaries contemporaneous with *The American Scene*—*The Question of Our Speech,* "The Speech of American Women," and "The Manners of American

Women"—James outlined the importance of speech, and particularly women's speech, for the reproduction of properly national social relations. In particular, James assailed what he considered their wholesale betrayal of the one bodily practice essential to the preservation of a civilized national culture: "the tone question" of the spoken English language. In *The Question of Our Speech*, James railed against having "handed over our property" to "the American Dutchman and Dago" so freely: "Our national use of vocal sound, in men and women alike, is slovenly—an absolute inexpert daub of unapplied tone" (41; 25). The increasingly heterogeneous character of the United States had resulted in yielding the pronunciation of the English language to those that James, in *The Bostonians*, had termed "the children of disappointment from beyond the seas" (316).

Seeking to redeem English from those who would speak most improperly, James placed "the labial question," or enunciation, at the heart of issues of U.S. nationality and civilization ("Speech" 179). The proper vocalization of language served as the primary measure of a national cultural consciousness. "A care for tone" indexed the very achievement, or lack thereof, of a national civilization (*Question* 13). As the sensitive index of "civilization," pronunciation of English and its representation within the realist novel revealed the slow accretion of habits, for James so evident in Europe and so tenuous in the United States, which demarcated a distinct national culture. Pronunciation marked the most fundamental tier of a series of bodily practices that made the civilized difference. Without proper speech, the very possibility of a national civilization became unthinkable. For James, the very ability to create "civilization" lay within the subtle degrees of sonic differences possible in proper speech, down to "the integrity of our syllables": "The syllables of our words, the tones of our voice, the shades of our articulation" served as "the most precious of our familiar tools" ("Speech" 196; 198). Proper speech, the most important of manners, taught how "to discriminate . . . to begin to prefer form to the absence of form, to distinguish color from the absence of color" (*Question* 36). Hinging upon making distinctions of form and color, speech structured the aesthetics of perception as well as the perception of aesthetics.

The discrete discriminations offered by the habit of proper enunciation formed the cornerstone for the other bodily habits of civilization. Providing the key cognitive ability that distinguished the civilized from the not civilized, proper pronunciation of English reproduced nationalized epistemologies of whiteness to reinscribe tenuous racial-colonial differences. The racial renewal of Anglo-Saxon civilization required the painstaking articulation of the "labial" to properly civilized bodily conduct: "The interest of tone is the interest of manners, and the interest of manners is the interest of morals, and the interest of morals is the interest of civilization" ("Speech" 199). Civilization for James was discrimination structured by language, but specifically discriminations whose time-worn paths became organized in historically specific ways as the second nature of manners precisely because they were rehearsed continuously in everyday life. These ensembles of proper speech habits and other manners were, for James, nation-building blocks. Recording "not only the history of the voice, but positively the history of the national character, almost the history of the people," speech and manners constituted the physical and psychic impressions of national culture that made all the relations of civilized life "hang together" (*Question* 34).

But if properly pronounced language enacted the epistemological possibilities of nation in its very utterance throughout a community of speakers, then mispronounced or accented English served as a reminder of the precarious state of that civilized national identity. As early as the 1882 short story "The Point of View," James had figured the impending "destruction of society" as the "vocal inflections of little news-boys" echoing in the voices of educated, "charming children" (536–37). A quarter-century later in *The American Scene*, James registered the "the piteous gasp" of a distressed English language in the "unprecedented accents" he heard spoken by immigrants inside an otherwise amenable New York East Side café (471). Within these "torture-rooms of the living idiom," James looked in vain "for some betrayal of a prehensile hook for the linguistic tradition as one had known it" (470–71). That the immigrant speakers within the café represented not "the mere mob" but "comparative civility" merely increased his "'lettered' anguish" at the seemingly inevitable disappearance of habits of discrimination that made for a distinctively "American" civilization (470).

Consonants disappeared and reappeared inappropriately, vowels drawled out of existence, and random yet stubbornly persistent noises attached themselves to the speech of even the educated, who, in apparent disregard for the differences between popular, political, and aesthetic discourses, talked "of vanilla-r-ice-cream, of California-r-oranges, of Cuba-r and Porto Rico, of Atlanta-r- in Calydon, and (very resentfully) of 'the very idea-r-of' any intimation that their performance and example in these respects may not be immaculate" (*Question* 27). Even teachers employed these maulings of speech, much to James's dismay. Instead of "Americanizing" immigrants through proper pronunciation, the democratic institutions of public education reflected the dominance of the million and the newspapers in this matter. It appeared to James that nothing was more apparent than the lack "of any positive tradition of speech, any felt consensus on the vocal, the lingual, the labial question, on the producing of the sound, on the forming of the word, of the discriminating of the syllable, on the preserving of the difference" that would prevent an alien takeover ("Speech" 179). Rather, U.S. national identity resided in the negation of discriminatory difference itself: even "as Nature abhors a vacuum, so it is of the genius of the American land and the American people to abhor, whenever may be, a discrimination" (*American Scene* 604).

Women in particular played central roles in guarding the nation's cognitive abilities to register "noticed differences" (*Question* 15). In his 1905 commencement address to the graduating class of women at Bryn Mawr College, published later that year as *The Question of Our Speech*, James exhorted the graduates to exercise their social influence as "models and missionaries, perhaps a little even martyrs, of the good cause" (52). Elite women such as these graduates did seem to make the best transmitters, as teachers and mothers, of vocal training, and, therefore, of national culture. Consequently, for James the great responsibility of transmitting "the very core of our social heritage," or "simply the idea of secure good manners," became a matter of "good breeding" (14). In the essay "The Speech of American Women," published a year after the Bryn Mawr address, James wrote that the speech of "well-bred" women "makes the demonstration—shows us what tone may do for intercourse and the beauty of life; what grace it may, even in the absence of other enrichment, contribute to the common colloquial act." It fell to women of the national elite to inculcate these nation-building practices in their children: "It is in their cords to give more effect to the intention" (180).

But if James appealed to the women of Bryn Mawr to help rescue the language, then it seemed to him for the most part that even, or especially, educated women insisted upon mauling the distinctions between sounds, "articulating as from sore mouths, all mumbling and whining and vocally limping and shuffling" ("Speech" 193). U.S. women spoke as they pleased rather than as they should, according to James, and did so because they had positively tied the freedom to do as they liked to the freedom to speak as they liked, "since the emancipation of the American woman would thereby be attested" ("Speech" 195). He attributed women's expanding ability to speak as they chose to the fundamentally gendered shift in social power after Reconstruction. Immediately after the Civil War, James found men in charge of national culture. Reviewing the British anthology *Modern Women* for the *Nation* in 1868, James asserted that women, far from setting the general moral tone of society or even offering a domestic alternative, merely reflected the world men made. When modern women "present an ugly picture," he wrote, men should "cast a glance at their own internal economy," since men "give the *ton*—they pitch the key" of all social relations (*Literary Criticism* 25).

But James's tone would change by the time he wrote the 1884 short story "A New England Winter." Upon his return to the United States, the Francophile expatriate Florimond Daintry would comment that Boston was "a city of women, in a country of women" (113). During the transatlantic absence of this Jamesian protagonist, the patriarchal ordering of U.S. society had apparently been superseded by a distinctly feminized regime. Shortly thereafter, Basil Ransom of *The Bostonians* would link women's speech to the downfall of the masculinist ability to discriminate for the sake of the nation's good, "to know and yet not fear reality, to look the world in the face and take it for what it is." Fearing the loss of this discriminatory technology to discern the elements of "a very queer and partly very base mixture," he launches a tirade against "the most damnable feminisation" of a "canting age": "The whole generation is womanised; the masculine tone is passing out of the world; it's a feminine, a nervous, hysterical, chattering, canting age, an age of hollow phrases and false delicacy and exaggerated solicitudes and coddled sensibilities, which, if we don't soon look out, will usher in the reign of mediocrity, of the feeblest and flattest and most pretentious that has ever been" (311). Echoing Ransom some twenty years later, James complained about the imperial stature of women in every social relation not that "of the stock-exchange or football field" ("Speech" 178). Men had become creatures of commerce after the Civil War, abdicating the field of "society," or the innumerable relationships that made "civilization" not solely a function of economics, in order to take care of business. Women occupied the vast social field thus abandoned and became "occupied in developing and extending her wonderful conquest" (*American Scene* 484). As a consequence, what James considered the social preeminence of women in the United States became the defining characteristic of national relations, "the sentence written largest in the American sky" (*American Scene* 639).[14]

Nothing for James would characterize the predominant situation of women more succinctly than the female voice in public arenas. While

James came to articulate these complaints most vocally in his commentaries written during and after his 1904–5 visit to the United States, he traced the genesis of his concern to the previous return visits of 1882–83, when he returned to bury his parents and subsequently finalized his plans to write *The Bostonians*. In "The Speech of American Women," James recalled how in the Boston of a quarter-century before, a city of "supremely conservative instincts," he was shocked by the "vociferous pupils" of a "seminary for young ladies" who hooted, howled, and "ingenuously shrieked and bawled to each other across the street and from its top to its bottom" (183–84). The problem for James was that this tone "was to be of use—that was the point—not in the gregarious life of labor, not in the rough world of the tenement, the factory, or the slum, the world unconscious of semitones, of vocal adjustments, but in the drawing-rooms and ball-rooms of the best society the country could show" (184–85).

If in *The Bostonians* Ransom could characterize a small group of feminists of the 1870s as a "herd of vociferating women" (46), then James would object in the 1907 article "The Manners of American Women" to the auditory uproar generated by a "bevy of young women . . . taking vociferous possession" of the Pullman car he occupied during his cross-country excursion. "From the point of view of tone and manner," these women flaunted the distinctions between "the great dusty public place" and their private "playground and maiden-bower" by "calling, giggling . . . shouting, flouncing, romping, [and] uproariously jesting" in the former ("Manners" 207–8). For James, the sight of these women reading newspapers and eating "the most violently heterogeneous food" marked the extent to which manners had already disappeared as a national civilized practice. Refusing to exercise "an elementary power or disposition to discriminate," a woman James observed eating let "the dauntless ladle plunge into the sherbet without prejudice to its familiarity with the squash, and struggle toward the custard while still enriched with the stuffing of the turkey" ("Manners" 227). This vision of "mixing salads with ices, fish with flesh, hot cakes with mutton chops, pickles with pastry, and maple syrup with everything" led James to comment:

> What law and what logic prevailed . . . at such a conceptions of a meal, and what presumption for felt congruities, for desired or perceived delicacies, in the other reaches of life, would it rouse in the mind of a visitor introduced for the first time to the spectacle? It was inevitable to feel, after a little, that speech and town and the terms of intercourse were, on the part

of these daughters of freedom, notions exactly as loose and crude as such notions of the nature of a repast. ("Manners" 227)

In other words, failing to make discreet choices about the foods they ate, U.S. women were unlikely to discriminate in other, more important matters of racial and cultural reproduction. All too apt to encourage biological, cultural, and linguistic miscegenation, U.S. women were for James "queens" without hierarchy. Supreme yet undiscriminating, their habits led to the "most violently heterogeneous" mixing of tastes, whether of food, newspapers, or companions.[15]

Having been fostered in an environment free of criticism, "'queens' on such easy terms" exercised their social power in an utterly unselfconscious and arbitrary way ("Manners" 238). Far from being too aristocratically "European" for U.S. democracy, the position of American women allowed them not just to ignore the relational nature of social life but to be unaware of it altogether. According to James, women were all too much the "most freely encouraged plant in our democratic garden" ("Speech" 167). Elite women from the United States apparently did not realize that "social, civil, conversational discipline consisted in having to recognize knowledge and competence and authority, accomplishment, experience and 'importance,' greater than one's own" ("Speech" 238). This willful ignorance precipitated a crisis in what James saw as the most conservative, and hence most important, social institution for the transmission of national culture: marriage. Holding that it was "easier to overlook any question of speech than to trouble about it" as it was "to snort or neigh, to growl or to 'meaow,' than to articulate and intonate," James wrote, "The conservative interest is really as indispensable for the institution of speech as for the institution of matrimony. Abate a jot of the quantity, and, much more, of the quality, of the consecration required, and we practically find ourselves emulating the beasts, who prosper as well without a vocabulary as without a marriage-service" (*Question* 47). But "the *related* state" was precisely what was missing for James in modern women. His fellow female travelers upon his cross-country journey "thus met and noted were of divorced and divorcing condition and intention—to which presumption their so frequently quite unhusbanded appearance much contributed" ("Manners" 243; emphasis in original). Rather than reflecting the Victorian domestic ideal of a moral, nurturing female domesticity, U.S. women represented a potential threat to the "secure transmission of manners" of a properly national civilization.

By disrupting the properly patriarchal paths of linguistic and cultural transmission, the uncouth manners and mouths of U.S. women threatened the racial renewal of Anglo-American civilization in its imperial dominance over the rest of the world. As U.S. women vocally refused what he considered their proper role in linguistically renewing the discriminatory epistemology of whiteness, James would attempt to shift the racial-cultural renewal of "national civilization" onto the novel itself. If a racialized pronunciation and perception could menace U.S. culture through the always unsecured bodies of white women, then for James the novel form possibly guaranteed its continuance by serving as the repository of the transmission process, both linguistically and historically. Even the combative "New Woman" of James's imagined dialogue in "The Speech of American Women" concedes that speech in novels (at least James's) is "syllabled" and "spelled out," to which he adds:

> Depend on it, dear young lady, these parts are there, theoretically, *all* sounded. The integrity of romance requires them without exception. And what are novels but the lesson of life? The retention of the covenanted parts is their absolute basis, without which they wouldn't for a moment hang together. The coherency of speech is the narrow end of the wedge they insert into our consciousness: the rest of their appeal comes only *after* that. (197)

Building national discriminations, the truly literary novel functioned to preserve national culture through the performance of linguistic distinctions. If national culture was constituted through the "wedge" of the novel, then novelistic language must not become contaminated by the guttural utterings of immigrant, working-class African Americans, or unruly white women. Even representing dialect in dialog, much less narrative, would become a national security threat. With the fate of Anglo-American civilization resting upon the Master's choice of words, James effectively transfers what had been white women's domestic role of cultural conservator to the properly aesthetic writer. Creating the racialized distinction between the national canon of serious literature and the ephemera of mass culture, James's realist aesthetic opened the high modernist abyss into which the racial uncertainties of empire can be thrown.

CHAPTER 3

The Hidden Power

Domesticity,
National Allegory,
and Empire in
Helen Hunt Jackson's *Ramona*

Thomas Henry Tibbles's 1881 novel *The Hidden Power* exposed what the Indian reform movement of the 1880s termed the notorious "Indian Ring"; however, in some way the title referred less to the corrupt system of Indian Bureau agents, frontier merchants, and opportunist politicians who robbed tribal nations and fomented white settler fears than to the "sweet and quiet" yet quite effective domestic influence wielded by a white female missionary. Overwhelmed by "the beauty of her countenance, the earnestness of her manner," the Missouri Indian Chief Red Iron discovers that the "weakness and gentleness of a delicate woman had conquered" his resistance to Christianity and civilization. Whereas punitive U.S. military campaigns and virtual imprisonment upon a reservation had failed to bring Red Iron and his tribal nation into the "pale of civilization," Mrs. Parkman "wielded a power stronger than the dictates of councils, or officers, or commissioners" in domesticating the recalcitrant savage. Giving up his own volition as well as tribal sovereignty, Red Iron tells her, "I will do anything you say"; indeed, the narrative notes, "Nothing would give Red Iron greater pleasure than to obey her" (93). Succeeding where physical coercion and political pressure had failed, Mrs. Parkman's domestic influence transformed Red Iron's tribalized resistance to U.S. imperialism into the seduction of personal submission to nationalized domestication.

Delicately disciplined by Mrs. Parkman's missionary manner, Red Iron instinctively casts off this anti-imperialist subjectivity for a suitably colonized one in a chapter aptly titled "A Woman's Conquest." In desiring to submit, Red Iron embodied the Indian reform movement's goals of domesticating rather than exterminating the Indians. Lobbying Congress, the president, and the public, Indian reform organizations orchestrated major media campaigns to effect drastic changes in federal policy towards tribal nations. Seeking to end U.S. policies they considered detrimental to the domestication of Indians, the Indian reform movement self-consciously modeled itself after abolitionism with its moral domestic appeal, even attracting former abolitionist activists such as Wendell Phillips and Lydia Maria Child.[1] Like the abolitionist movement of the earlier part of the century, the Indian policy reformers sought to mobilize the public by presenting policy issues in novels, newspaper editorials, pamphlets, testimonials, speeches, conferences, and other media.

Making explicit the connections between U.S. colonial policy and domesticity, Indian reform novels figured the invisible moral influence of white women as the answer to the "Indian question." If the mutual determination of the (white) national and the (nonwhite) foreign within Manifest Destiny had worked to replicate those registers of colonial representation, post-Reconstruction domestic discourses yielded an inclusive, liberal form of colonial difference. The white women of the Indian reform movement inhabited less a perfect duplication of the enabling public/domestic dichotomy than a subtle transformation of the relationship between social actors and the colonial state that formally delineated the gendered and racialized limits of social agency.

The discourse of separate spheres, as has often been pointed out, obscures the complicated and conflicted ways middle- and upper-class white women lived within the patriarchal operation of familial life and the masculinized public endeavors of political economy, particularly affairs of state. Rather than simply stabilize the ideology of separate spheres, the long history of these women's engagement within social movements whose ultimate aim had been state intervention ("reform") often resulted in a transformed relationship between the state, the groups imagined as beneficiaries of reform, and the domestic reformers, who themselves based their justification for moral interventions within the public sphere upon the very conceptual binary their actions were abridging. The nineteenth-century reform movements in which domesticity played a key role, and specifically the Indian reform movement of the 1880s and 1890s, can be seen as the double-dealing movement of modernity in which colonial administration was imagined by reformers as a liberative project whereby uncivilized Indians could be redeemed through the civilizing domesticity of white women.

Indian reform novels challenge not only the binaristic configuration of separate spheres but also our understanding of the role of civil society in formulating the parameters of colonial administration. While the state may ultimately arbitrate the legal terms of colonial difference, implementation of such policies often depended upon the representational trends initiated within reform movements and civil society as a whole. Civil society composed and debated the direction of state policy, and, in particular, discourses and practices of domesticity often shaped the discursive parameters through which official policy, and the nature of colonial difference such policies assumed, could be imagined and practiced. In other words, the cultural practices of U.S. imperialism not only generated and sustained imperialist subjectivities and ideologies necessary to the expansion and maintenance of the U.S. empire but also coalesced the imperial nation's civil society as the thought laboratory within which the collective logic of colonial rule could be formulated. The national debate over the "Indian question" during the 1880s served as such a site. The Indian reform movement coalesced the option of "domestication" by reorganizing Manifest Destiny's logic of national exclusion into post-Reconstruction domesticity's logic of national inclusion.

Indian reform novels such as *The Hidden Power* and especially Helen Hunt Jackson's *Ramona* (1884) emphasize domesticity's centrality to the production of late nineteenth-century U.S. imperial discourses and nation-building practices. Despite the Indian reform movement's small number of activists, its largely New England–based constituency of well-placed, well-educated political, religious, and academic elites resulted in cultural and political influence far beyond the relatively small numbers of activists officially registered in the three main organizations (the Lake Mohonk Conference of the Friends of the Indian, the Indian Rights Association, and the Women's National Indian Association). Within these groups, a dedicated base of upper-middle-class white women posited domestic influence as the gentle force that calmed a native resistance only tentatively contained upon reservations. The aesthetics of domestic influence in the public policy–oriented Indian reform novel thus emerged as a key paradigm for formulating federal policy towards tribal nations.

Challenging current scholarly notions of domestic discourses as simply engaged in the politics of anti-patriarchal resistance or simply disengaged from the racialized practices of U.S. imperialism, Indian reform novels demonstrate the complex and multiple determinations of agency and subjectivity within the post-Reconstruction context. Intertwining the discourse of domesticity as configured within white nationalism with the question of the colonial management of nonwhite populations, Indian reform novels highlight the critical need to articulate two areas of scholarship—studies of domesticity and studies of imperialism—that have typically been theorized separately. Far from positing an unbridgeable chasm between the domestic and public spheres, these novels explicitly elaborated their synergy in imperial endeavors. If previous scholarly considerations have failed to take into account domesticity's imperial entanglements, recent efforts by Amy Kaplan, Lora Romero, Karen Sánchez-Eppler, Laura Wexler, and others have provided a much-needed theoretical corrective for the study of U.S. imperial culture through their examinations of nineteenth-century housekeeping manuals, missionary tracts, and novels, domestic and otherwise.[2] I wish to contribute to this ongoing conversation by focusing upon the role of domesticity in placing the civilizing aesthetics of domestic influence at the heart of U.S. imperial practices.[3]

"Manifest Domesticity," as Kaplan has usefully termed the mutually informing nexus of U.S. imperialist and domestic discourses, articulated the political economy of empire through the delimiting of national citizenship.[4] Manifest Domesticity coordinated the imperial incorporation of foreign territories and peoples with the domestic whiteness that preserved, renewed, and guaranteed what Partha Chatterjee has termed the rule of colonial difference, or the preservation of an imagined, nigh-unbridgeable difference (often but not always or simply racialized) between the colonizer and the colonized.[5] Each discourse justified the other. U.S. imperialism fueled domesticity's expansive tendencies by annexing savage lands in dire need of civilization, while domesticity provided the racial syntax necessary for delineating the ever-expanding boundaries of the white nation.[6] The imperial logic of U.S. territorial expansion entailed the convulsively violent annexation of not only foreign land but nonwhite peoples as well, introducing a threat to white national identity. Turning "an imperial nation into a home by producing and colonizing specters of the foreign that lurk inside and outside its ever shifting borders," Manifest Domesticity (re)produced the white nation even as each territorial expansion challenged the nation's whiteness ("Manifest Domesticity" 602). Keeping the nation white, Manifest Domesticity performed the cultural work of border patrolling suited to U.S. imperialism during the era of Manifest Destiny, starting with the forced removal of tribal nations during the 1830s, through the annexation of the northern half of Mexico following the U.S.-Mexican War and until the Civil War.

As both anticipation and response to the unwanted presence of people of color in conquered territories, Manifest Domesticity fixed upon the deportation of nonwhite peoples from the national imaginary of home. Kaplan highlights this convergence of domestic and political discourses in her discussion of Sarah Josepha Hale's campaign to make Thanksgiving a national holiday. As Kaplan relates, Hale's proposal required state sanction; for Hale, this holiday would consolidate the white home and the white nation (one and the same project) through the expulsion of black people, free or slave, to Liberia.[7] In this instance, President Lincoln's proclamation establishing the holiday in 1863 did not precipitate the desired deportations. Nonetheless Hale's campaign for Thanksgiving, like Harriet Beecher Stowe's abolitionist novel *Uncle Tom's Cabin*, called for state action to fulfill domestically imagined projects of racial segregation discursively cast as projects of racial liberation (whether expressly white or black, as in the respective cases of Hale and Stowe).[8] As Manifest Domesticity's preferred method for achieving national (white) liberation, deportation would ensure that nonwhite peoples would remain foreign to citizenship even if not literally expelled from the nation. Conquered or exploited, African captives, Asian immigrants, Mexicans, and Indians remained outside the mutually constitutive, homely national discourses of domesticity and imperial law.[9]

Yet limiting the cultural work of Manifest Domesticity to (re)creating U.S. white homes or to legitimating imperial conquest underplays the era's continuous making of colonial difference (and hence colonial practice) through the terms of domesticity itself. Imagining the imperial nation as a home, and whiteness as the key determinant of domestic inclusion, Manifest Domesticity served as a key site within U.S. civil society wherein the practices of colonial administration were formulated and debated, thus generating potential solutions to the specific problems of colonial administration. Such an articulation, as suggested by Indian reform novels, requires rethinking the politics of domesticity within the gendered conditions of imperial agency and national subjectivity. As Louise Newman has documented, U.S. feminist movements in the nineteenth century must be understood within a global colonial context in which arguments for the civil rights of white women were formulated through a domestic understanding of colonial difference.[10]

Helen Hunt Jackson was not active in suffragist or other women's rights movements, yet nonetheless she helped to open new avenues of access to the public sphere. This irony reflects the common discursive construction of civilization that created such opportunities for elite white women at this historical moment. Framed as a moral issue for the nation, the Indian question enabled Jackson, among others, access to public social agency scarcely afforded to any woman.[11] The very conditions of *Ramona*'s production were tied not only to Jackson's understanding of her role within the Indian reform movement but also to her ability to negotiate entry into official colonial administration upon that basis. Articulating the question of domesticity through the national "problem" of civilizing Indians, *Ramona* uniquely encapsulates the racially differentiated construction of colonial agency through the gendered assumptions of civilizational development by which white women justified the expansion of their roles in public matters.

As Priscilla Wald has demonstrated, tribal nations had long posed a serious conceptual challenge to U.S. national identity as alternative communities that, even if construed as "domestic dependent nations," nonetheless threatened to collapse the very construction of colonial difference that legitimated U.S. imperialism.[12] Insofar as tribal nations such as the Cherokee appropriated and transformed the textual forms of U.S. nationhood (e.g., a constitution) in order to collectively assert tribal sovereignty in the face of U.S. imperialism, these acts of colonial mimicry disrupted popular discourses of Indian savagery and hence the very rationale for white dispossession of tribal nations. As Wald put it, tribal nations "represented the threat offered by the proximity of an alternative collectivity" (43). In the face of Indian resistance throughout the nineteenth century, the debate over the "Indian question" concerned the nature of colonial difference and the policies resulting from a particular understanding of that difference.

Federal policy towards tribal nations had historically combined strategies of treaty making, removal, military conquest, and assimilation (although not always equally, simultaneously, or consistently). By the late 1870s, only the latter two policies remained.[13] Despite guerrilla resistance, most tribal nations had been militarily defeated by the 1880s. With no lands beyond the reach of white settlers to practice Manifest Domesticity's solution of Indian removal, the "Indian question" became a matter of "the stern alternative" of "extermination or civilization," according to Secretary of the Interior Carl Schurz in 1881 (7). This conceptual binary reworked the hoary colonial trope of the vanishing Indian into the question of just how best to accomplish the disappearance of Indians, who, despite all predictions of inevitable, natural demise, remained stubbornly persistent. The continued cultural viability of tribal nations within the reservation system begged the question of Indian disappearance. Even as U.S. policy towards tribal nations oscillated between de facto genocide and programmatic incorporation, the Indian reform movement coalesced during the late 1870s and early 1880s to influence public policy towards the latter position.

Insofar as the shared aim of making Indians vanish joined Indian haters and Indian reformers in their common vision of U.S. imperial rule over tribal nations, the different positions within the "Indian question" indexed distinct conceptions of Indian racialization. The apparent difference between widespread popular support for extermination and the domestication offered by the Indian reform movement lay largely in the specific approach to be used in colonial management. Advocates of extermination held that the nature of Indian difference was racially immutable and resolutely antagonistic.[14] In contrast, Indian reform novels sought to effect changes in federal policy by displacing the popular notion of the inhuman savage with the anthropological concept of the tractable primitive. Opposing those who would kill Indians upon the basis of absolute racial difference, Indian policy reformers thus characterized the nature of colonial difference as developmentally cultural, giving the more advanced white race the moral duty to educate primitive Indians into civilization.

However, a key conceptual problem for the Indian reform movement lay in the disjuncture between the racialized knowledge being produced by key segments of civil society about the cultural superiority of the white race and the actual state practice of acknowledging and fulfilling treaty obligations (even if more honored in the breach than in the observance). Manifest domesticity generated the racial differences that consolidated "the national" and "the foreign," yet tribal nations presented the specter of nonwhite nations that in certain key respects held, and demanded, equal footing in treaties with the allegedly superior white nation. The racially foreign comprised a nonwhite nationality, thereby emphasizing the modern, state-to-state nature of the complex relationship between the United States and tribal nations.[15]

In effect, the Indian policy reformers sought to transform the political relationship between the United States and tribal nations into the evolutionary relationship between civilized nations and primitive races by positing Indians as culturally less advanced peoples who should be educated into modernity rather than as modern rivals whose national sovereignty posed a significant conceptual threat to U.S. nationalism. As the burden of white folks and the measure of its civilization, the moral imperative of domesticating the Indian united the homework of the domestic sphere with the empire building of the public sphere in making U.S. citizens out of primitive savages. The reformers' emphasis upon assimilation transformed Manifest Domesticity's white nationalism to suit the new problems of colonial management in the post-Reconstruction era of national consolidation. In advocating assimilation over genocide or removal, Indian reform novels chart the transformation of domesticity-influenced colonial difference from the abolitionist emphasis upon the expulsion of racial difference during the 1850s to the Indian reform movement's advocacy of incorporation during the 1880s.

Nowhere is this revised imperialist cultural work of domesticity more suggestively apparent than in Helen Hunt Jackson's 1884 historical romance *Ramona*, the best known of the Indian reform novels and a steady best-seller for over five decades. Figuring the domestication of Indians as the homework of white women, Jackson would specifically employ the narrative strategies of domestic novels to imagine the possibility of civilizing Indians into a harmonious multiracial nation. In the "privilidged character" of Aunt Ri, Jackson depicts a white woman's housework as performing the crucial domestic task of nation building (412). Aunt Ri, a white Southerner who overcomes her prejudices against Indians, serves as Jackson's example of racial tolerance. A rag carpet of what Aunt Ri calls the "hit-er-miss" pattern emerges as the novel's metaphor for a reformed United States that made no invidious distinctions among its inhabitants on account of race. In this pattern, there are "no set stripes or regular alternation of colors, but ball after ball of the indiscriminately mixed tints, woven back and forth, on a warp of a single color" (410). Claiming she had never seen a "hit-er-miss" pattern "thet wa'n't pooty," Aunt Ri delights "in the constant variety in it, the unexpectedly harmonious blending of the colors" (410). The cultural work of integrating all citizens, actual or potential, regardless of race, appears as the task and result of white domesticity's housework. Indeed, the intentionality of invidiously racialized projects can only produce results that displease. According to Aunt Ri, those who "hed 'em planned aout" from "ther warp" to "ther stripes" were always "orful diserpynted when they cum ter see 't done" (410).

Quite unlike Henry James's cultured refusal of dialect as a literary strategy, Jackson used the Tennessee "Pike" dialect to mark Aunt Ri's distance from the social norms of the Eastern reformist elite as well as from those of the Southern belle of the former plantation class. By having the working-class Southerner Aunt Ri articulate the principles of a racially democratic project of nation building, Jackson ties the Reconstruction-era project of incorporating the freedmen into the nation as citizens with the post-Reconstruction project of domesticating Indians into U.S. citizenship. Yet the coalescing of Jim Crow discourses of violent black male sexuality specifically precluded white women from exercising a domesticating influence that would require a close proximity to such imagined dangers. In contrast, the Indian captivity narrative, which emphasized the dangerous potential for the interracial rape of white women by Indian men, had ceased to invoke a generalized sense of racial terror at a time when tribal nations had been largely defeated and Indians were mostly encountered in dime novels or ethnographies. Domestication by white women could thus work in the latter case, but not the former. Avoiding such imagined racial violence, the Indian reform project of civilizing savages could imaginatively unite Northern and Southern white women for the imperial task of nation building after the unsisterly divisions of the Civil War and Reconstruction.

Like Aunt Ri's weaving, Jackson's writing attempted to imagine the domestic incorporation of Indians as citizens even as that incorporation united North and South in the nation's imperial mission. In this sense, *Ramona* reorients the nation-building dynamics of the romance of reunion. Rather than explicitly highlight the reunification of North and South, the novel screens the drama of racial equality that so plagued Reconstruction upon the picturesque love story between the Californiana mestiza Ramona and the Diegueño Indian Alessandro Assis. Free of the taint of miscegenation (because already performed in the Mexican past), this transposition serves to critique a biologically racialized order that would not assimilate Indians and mixed bloods who have already internalized the rational precepts of civilization, and who have (even if only by necessity) renounced tribal relations. In the context of the mid-1880s, *Ramona* offered a liberal alternative to Jim Crow segregation and to the outright genocide of Indians. The assimulationist aesthetics of post-Reconstruction domesticity imagined diversity in union, and harmony in diversity.[16]

If within the masculinist discourse of U.S. imperialism, the Indians were destined to disappear before white civilization in a literal sense, then, within the sentimental discourse of domesticity, the savages were to disappear figuratively as the objects of white women's civilizing activities.

This transformation was formulated in explicit relation to a change in the legal status of Indians. Through the alchemy of domestic influence, racial tutelage would transmute lesser breeds without the law into citizens subject to nation's law. The education of Indians into civilization necessarily entailed the normalization of their status vis-à-vis the federal government. Whereas extermination would ensure that no Indian would ever become a citizen, domestication made that eventuality the measure of the nation's civilization itself. Indian reform novels aligned domestication and emergent anthropological theories of civilization by linking U.S. law, private property, and proper gender relations over and against the lawlessness of the uncivilized, undifferentiated, but sovereign tribes.

Basing their arguments upon recently popularized anthropological theories of the evolutionary development of human culture through the universal stages of savagery, barbarism, and civilization, Indian policy reformers claimed that savage and barbarous Indians were indeed capable of achieving civilization with the proper guidance from the already civilized white races. The racialized pedagogical disciplining of Indian minds would replace the fatal punishment of Indian bodies. In contrast to extermination, domestication would allow white recognition of Indian humanity by remapping a static hierarchy of racial difference onto a flexible historical trajectory of cultural development.[17] The reformers sought to reform not only U.S. Indian policy but Indians themselves by reinscribing colonial difference not (strictly) as a matter of race, but as a question of culture. Making the question of colonial difference a matter of degree rather than of kind, this representational shift relied upon domestic influence both for its popular dissemination as discursive knowledge constructing its theoretical object ("the Indian") and for its perceived efficacy as a colonial policy to manage said object. In wishing to emphasize benevolent assimilation over genocidal conquest, the reformers repudiated popular imperial discourses of irredeemable, inhuman Indian savagery. They instead advocated the paternalistic instruction of the now dependent, child-like, and primitive Indians in a bid to demonstrate that the policy of racial tutelage would better reflect the civilized's collective fitness for colonial rule than would outright genocide.

In essence, the domestic influence of Indian reform novels would work to make Indians vanish by figuring them as colonial mimics. What Homi Bhabha terms the discourse of colonial mimicry imagined the elimination of colonial difference, here taken as a developmental cultural difference existing prior to and outside of the colonial relationship, as the Enlightenment-inspired goal of colonial management.[18] Understood not as the functioning of colonial power/knowledge networks but as the rationale for the colonial situation itself, colonial mimicry entailed the elimination of the Other's cultural difference through racial tutelage. The Indian reform movement advocated Indian assimilation into the nation rather than their expulsion (figuratively or literally) from it, thus unambiguously raising the question of colonial governance of nonwhite peoples in the U.S. context. Partha Chatterjee outlines the three possibilities for colonial governance arising from Enlightenment narratives:

> One is that [the universality of the modern institutions of self-government] must apply in principle to all societies irrespective of historical or cultural specificities. The second is that the principle is inescapably tied to the specific history and culture of Western societies and cannot be exported elsewhere; this implies a rejection of the universality of the principle. The third is that the historical and cultural differences, although an impediment in the beginning, can be eventually overcome by a suitable process of training and education. The third position, therefore, while admitting the objection raised by the second, nevertheless seeks to restore the universality of the principle. (18)

Chatterjee's characterization of the colonial predicament concerning the universality of liberal technologies of governance and Bhabha's formulation of colonial mimicry intersect in the following question: what is the implied relationship between the mode of colonial governance vis-à-vis modern disciplinary technologies of liberalism and the shape of the civil society that government must rule? In other words, what necessary correspondence, if any, must there be between culture and government? In the context of the late nineteenth-century U.S. colonial situation, the discourse of civilization articulated these fundamental linkages. Otherwise known as *la mision civilatrice*, benevolent assimilation, or the white man's burden, the third proposition offered perhaps the greatest flexibility in implementing the colonial state's regimes of disciplinary power to distinguish colonizer from colonized in that the rule of colonial difference could be explicitly articulated through Enlightenment discourses of nationalist liberalism.[19] Even as the (male) populations of the colonial metropoles were increasingly interpolated as citizen-subjects through state disciplinary regimes and liberal discourses throughout the nineteenth century, the modern state could construct colonial difference through the same liberal practices that held out the promise of full social agency (i.e., citizenship) rather than exclude on the basis of immutable racial difference. The project of normalizing the status of "natives" could then be relegated to an always-to-be-completed status even while allowing incremental changes.[20]

As a key discursive site for the Indian reform movement, the Indian reform novel, *Ramona* in particular, coordinated the proliferating array of residual and emergent colonial representational practices (such as the travel narrative, the colonial administrative report, the missionary tract, the ethnographic analysis, the vanishing native story) within a moralistic narrative. Indian reform models made coherent the myriad modes of narrating colonial difference, or, in different terms, the common sense of U.S. imperialist subjectivities, discourses, and practices, to a white middle-class reading public even while reconfiguring the possibilities of social agency for white women.

The Aesthetics of Reform

Reviewing *Ramona* in the September 1886 issue of the *North American Review*, former Reconstruction-era judge and prominent Northern liberal Albion Tourgée praised Jackson's historical romance as "unquestionably the best novel yet produced by an American woman" (246). The author of two novels—*A Fool's Errand* (1879) and *Bricks Without Straw* (1880)—critical of Northern acquiescence to Southern white supremacy, Tourgée defended Jackson's novel from imagined realist critics who would "sneeringly" object to this historical romance as a "novel with a purpose" (251). Unlike realist narratives that incessantly belabored the self-reflexive process of artistic creation, the subject of Tourgée's book review betrayed "no trace of effort" in its "unconscious vigor." In contrast to the obsessively self-conscious assertion of artistic agency within realist novel, *Ramona* was "so thoroughly done that the hand of the artist is never seen in it" (246). Insofar as the art of *Ramona* appeared to be "artless" in the realist sense, Tourgée characterized the novel less as the intentional product of Jackson's literary labor than as the "harmonious" expression of an instinctual genius of "sympathy." Linking domesticity to writing, Jackson seemed to have "instinctively" written the novel "with that unconscious art which characterizes true genius." Tourgée found "a wondrous glow of perfect knowledge" surrounded the text's "clearness of conception, depth of coloring, purity of tone, individuality and pleasing contrast of characters, and intensity of emotion." Jackson's "intimate acquaintance and perfect sympathy for the life she describes" almost bridged the gap between fact and fiction: "Scenes, incidents, characters—all reveal the fact that the author has not only an intellectual appreciation of their existence, but that knowledge which comes from an observation so close and sympathetic as to amount almost to experience" (251). Far from practicing art for art's sake, Jackson (best known as the poet "H.H." to the reading public) had harnessed this pleasing literary aestheticism to delineating social relations long erased in the U.S. popular imagination.

Depicting the "conflict of jarring civilizations," *Ramona* made visible to Tourgée the historical connections that had gone completely unexamined in previous literary representations of the "greedy, glittering fact" known as California (248). "[N]ot altogether a tale of *our* California," *Ramona* brought to life the California erased by literary representations of the Golden State as "the gold-digger's paradise, the adventurer's Eden, the speculator's El Dorado" (247). In telling the story of those displaced economically and literarily by "this modern miracle we call California," this novel recalled for Tourgée "the civilization of New Spain" and its sad ruins still visible as "the Indian's lost inheritance and the Spaniard's desolated home" (249). If the history of the Californios and the indigenous peoples had been forgotten by "a fresher and stronger social, political, and religious development" of a "grasping, arrogant, self-worshipping multitude" that trampled "ruthlessly, because unconsciously" upon these "two decaying civilizations," then *Ramona* would "awaken thought on the part of her countrymen" by refocusing national attention upon "the Indian question" as a moral and political problem for the nation (248; 247; 253).

Jackson herself desired that her audience fall under the artless domestic influence of *Ramona*. In particular, she wanted readers to consider the national failure to enact what historian Frederick Hoxie has called a final promise to the Indians: assimilation.[21] Her previous effort in this vein, the factual exposé *A Century of Dishonor*, had not generated enough political momentum to push reform measures through Congress. A product of long hours spent pouring over government archives, this 1881 treatise catalogued the U.S. government's flagrant violation of treaties as well as numerous examples of atrocities committed by whites upon Indians. Hoping to sway Congress, Jackson sent every senator and representative a copy of *A Century of Dishonor* embossed with a quotation from Benjamin Franklin upon the blood-red cover: "Look upon your hands! They are stained with the blood of your relations" (qtd. in Mathes 36).

But Jackson found that the moral outrage of history had no efficacy in swaying a public indifferent to the cause of justice for a despised racial community. *A Century of Dishonor*, wrote Jackson in 1885, "failed to realize my hopes. I fear few have read it, except those that did not need to" (*Letters* 340). Jackson attributed the treatise's failure to produce meaningful public support for reform to a disjunction between the nation's morals and the nation's reading habits. The public read for personal pleasure, not for moral enlightenment. Convinced that "people will read a novel when they will not read serious books," Jackson sought with the historical romance *Ramona* to reach the mass market of leisure readers who had ignored the elaborate legal arguments and the impassioned pleas for justice that characterized *A Century of Dishonor* (*Letters* 298). Jackson would write *Ramona* as a fictional historical romance that would teach even as it delighted: "What I wanted to do, was to draw a picture so winning and alluring in the beginning of the story, that the reader would become thoroughly interested in the characters before he dreamed of what was before him:—and would have swallowed a big dose of information on the Indian Question, without knowing it" (*Letters* 337). Representing "the consummate triumph of art" in *Ramona*, the Señora Moreno's invisible yet complete domestic rule of the Moreno household figures what Jackson hoped would be the novel's effectiveness in bringing about Indian policy reform: "To attain one's end in this way is the consummate triumph of art. Never to appear as a factor in the situation; to be able to wield other men, as instruments, with the same direct and implicit response to will that one gets from a hand or a foot,—this is to triumph, indeed: to be as nearly controller and conqueror of Fates as fate permits" (12).

Ramona relates the trials and tribulations of the mestiza title character in Reconstruction-era Southern California. Raised as the stepdaughter of the Morenos, a wealthy Californio ranchero family, Ramona Ortegna is kept ignorant of her mixed-blood parentage by the strict widow Señora Moreno, whose only son, Felipe, secretly loves the teenaged ward. Ramona only learns of her Indian mother when she falls in love with Alessandro Assis, a Diegueño Indian from the *ranchería* of Temecula. Ramona and Alessandro elope after meeting with Señora Moreno's disapproval, and, during their married life in various Indian villages, Ramona readily adjusts to the life she always felt she should have had as an Indian woman. Yet white squatters and settlers continually drive Alessandro and Ramona off traditionally Indian lands. With no recourse to U.S. law, the couple must constantly migrate to evermore marginal lands to escape white persecution. Even a remote mountainside refuge proves inadequate to shut out tragedy brought about by racial injustice. Alessandro and Ramona's first child dies of grossly negligent medical care by an Indian Agency doctor, and Alessandro himself is unjustly shot as a horse thief, leaving the grieving Ramona and their second child in the care of Felipe. Disgusted by thieving gringos, Felipe removes to Mexico, taking the long-suffering Ramona along as his bride and adopting her daughter as his own.

While clearly the outcome of *Ramona* involves not the national incorporation of Indians but rather their expulsion from national space, Jackson hoped that readers would interpret this conclusion as a moral wrong to be righted, as an outrage committed "In the Name of the Law" (her first and preferred title for the narrative), which demonstrated the need to reform said law (*Letters* 307). For Jackson, generating public goodwill for Indians against popular discourses of inhuman, indelible Indian savagery required repudiating older narrative forms that still shaped the U.S. imaginary. Jackson recalled how her own imaginings of Indians had been informed by sensationalist accounts of white homes under savage siege: "I grew up with my sole idea of the Indian derived from the account of Massacres. It was one of childish terrors that Indians would come in the night, & kill us" (*Letters* 330). While the yet more dreadful captivity narrative lurked behind fears of being murdered by Indians, Jackson implicitly recognized that the most popular U.S. discourses about Indians—the massacre and captivity narratives—advocated Indian extermination by propagating a sense of inhuman red deviltry, of absolute racial (and hence moral) difference.

Turning to the domestic therapy that would restore the moral sense of the body politic, Jackson wrote about her intensions for *Ramona* in an 1885 letter: "In my *Century of Dishonor* I tried to attack people's consciences directly, and they would not listen. Now I have sugared the pill, and it remains to be seen if it will go down" (*Letters* 341). Casting fiction writing as home remedy, Jackson hoped to teach the reading public what Aunt Ri learns about Indian humanity during the course of the narrative. After meeting Ramona and Alessandro, she discovers how mistaken her knowledge about Indians, gathered primarily "from newspapers, and from a book or two of narratives of massacres," really is. Seeing firsthand how much the Indian family is like her own, Aunt Ri admits, "I've got a lesson'n the subjeck uv Injuns" (335). Domestic influence would lead readers to join Aunt Ri in repudiating widespread discourses of Indian deviltry and instead acknowledge Indians as fellow human beings in a less civilized but amicable and tractable state.

In this sense, the narrative strategy of Indian reform novels was also the political strategy of the Indian reform movement. Only appearing artless, this artful domestic influence formed the central representational strategy for those involved in righting the nation's racial wrongs during the nineteenth century. Abolitionists and their successors in Indian reform drew upon the nation's tradition of liberal dissent generally and particularly upon the moral suasion of women's domestic sensibilities in mobilizing citizens to end inhumane practices against wronged racial groups. Indian reform movement writers followed their abolitionist precursors in employing indirect moral influence to generate public backing for their reforms. Casting Indians and Africans as the saintly victims of rapacious, corrupt, and decidedly un-Christian whites, whether pre-Emancipation plantation owners and overseers or post-Reconstruction Indian agents and settlers, *Ramona* and its abolitionist precursor, Stowe's *Uncle Tom's Cabin*, would exercise domestic influence hidden in narrative form to achieve their ends.

"If I could write a story that would do for the Indian a thousandth part what *Uncle Tom's Cabin* did for the Negro, I would be thankful for the rest of my life," Jackson wrote to the editor of the *Atlantic Monthly* in May 1883 (*Letters* 258). In the spirit of Stowe, Jackson would start writing *Ramona* seven months later in a bid to win public support for the small but burgeoning Indian reform movement of which she had been an early proponent. In wishing to emulate the success of Stowe's novel in changing the terms of the national discussion, Jackson acknowledged the power of women's domestic influence within the public sphere for outlining the moral issues facing the nation and for mobilizing the nation to redress racial injustice. If the Indians were not slaves in the way the freedmen had been, nonetheless the imperative to redress this "stain of a century of dishonor" upon the national consciousness in its dealings with the tribal nations would be even greater since the U.S. government itself had been directly responsible for what appeared to be the Indians' imminent extinction (*Century of Dishonor* 31). Casting the Indian reform movement as the successor of the abolitionist movement, Jackson would employ the same moral power of domestic influence in *Ramona* that Stowe had so strategically drawn upon for *Uncle Tom's Cabin*.[22]

Both novels worked to create moral outrage at the inhumane treatment of human beings unjustly reduced legally to something other than human. Like the abolitionist movement before the Civil War, the Indian reform movement based its moral appeal upon having the fundamental humanity of a racialized group, unjustly reviled nationwide, acknowledged through governmental intervention. Legislation to protect the civil rights of these groups precisely indicated the nation's commitment to recognizing that humanity. Seeking in this way to alleviate the unjust sufferings of an aggrieved racial Other, Stowe and Jackson wrote their respective novels to move the nation into sympathetic recognition of enslaved Africans and defeated Indians as part of humanity, a sentiment they hoped would translate into the full recognition of the African and the Indian as persons before the law. Reform might ultimately be a moral imperative and not a political one, yet the morality of the domestic sphere could only be enacted in the public sphere.

As the paramount goal of abolitionists and Indian policy reformers, the recognition and protection of the legal personhood of the African or the Indian meant no less than the extension of American freedom to those explicitly not free. Indians might not be slaves, but, like slaves before Emancipation, had no standing before the law as legal "persons." Whereas slaves, as property, had no personhood per se in a pre-Emancipation court of law, Indians, as members of "domestic dependent nations" set apart from the United States, could not seek the protection of the federal courts. Legally recognized as a person, the African could be protected from enslavement. Likewise, the Indian, while not enslaved as chattel, could be freed from the tyranny of the reservation system, which, in Jackson's opinion, left the Indian "far worse off than the average slave ever was" despite being "a far nobler creature" (*Letters* 135).[23] The Civil War and Reconstruction had seen the formal goals of the abolitionists—emancipation and civil rights for African Americans stemming from the recognition of legal personhood—largely accomplished, even if by the 1880s those results were being rendered increasingly tenuous with the cultural and legal consolidation of Jim Crow.

In contrast, the "Indian question," while even older than the "Negro question," had continued to vex the nation. Manifest Destiny had precipitated open warfare between various tribal nations and the U.S. government, culminating in the so-called Indian Wars in the two decades following the Civil War. During Reconstruction and afterwards, tribal nations posed serious obstacles to settlement and commercial development of the intermountain West. The reformers' appeal for the nation to recognize the humanity of Indians had been greatly complicated by the intense military conflict over the resources of land and cultural survival, which during the decades of westward expansion had produced what Herman Melville, in his novel *The Confidence-Man*, termed "the metaphysics of Indian-hating" as a national structure of feeling (192). Even as *Ramona* was being serialized in the *Christian Union* beginning in May 1884, the U.S. military waged active campaigns against the Chiricahua Apache band lead by Geronimo. But as the tribal nations approached military defeat, reformers maintained that the federal government had largely suspended its outright killing of Indians with a slower but equally effective method of insuring their extinction: the reservation system. Forced into a humiliating dependency upon the very government they had resisted for so long, tribal nations had been settled upon agriculturally marginal lands and placed into the tenacious grip of unscrupulous Indian agents who grew rich siphoning off treaty-negotiated allotments of government goods. Government statistics that recorded the steady decline of reservation populations only confirmed this narrative of the vanishing Indian.[24]

During the military conflict between the United States and the tribal nations of the Great Plains and the Southwest throughout the 1870s, the "Indian question" seemed to be largely the frontier concern of Westerners who imagined themselves in imminent danger of Indian attack. Not until the well-publicized flight and trial of the Ponca Nation did the legal relationship between the tribal nations and the federal government come under sustained press scrutiny. The Ponca, ever on peaceful terms with whites, had been forcibly driven from their treaty reservation on tribal homelands in northern Nebraska to marginal lands in Indian Territory by a federal bureaucratic error that had assigned their reservation lands in a subsequent treaty to their old enemy the Sioux. One-third of the tribal nation had died during and after the removal, and, upon the deaths of all but one of his children, Ponca Chief Standing Bear decided to return with a small band of followers to the tribal homelands. While staying with the closely related Omaha nation, Standing Bear and the other Ponca were arrested by U.S. Army Brigadier General George Crook for leaving the Indian Territory reservation without federal permission.

The 1879 decision of U.S. federal judge Elmer S. Dundy in the *Standing Bear v. Crook* case established a new precedent in interpreting the Indian as subject to the jurisdiction of the U.S. legal system, and thus ushered in a new era of the extension of the nation's power over the tribal nations. Dundy ruled that Standing Bear and his fellow Ponca prisoners were entitled to the issuance of writs of habeas corpus, and thus release from military custody. The decision hinged upon the key legal finding of the case: "That an Indian is a Person within the meaning of the laws of the United States" (Tibbles, *Standing Bear* 110). Dundy concluded that the meaning of "person" in the wording of U.S. statutes was not reducible to "citizen," but rather included any human being. Granting that "even an Indian" landed in the latter, more expansive definition of "person," Dundy found that Indians subsequently had the right of due process of law under the Fourteenth Amendment (100). Introducing this finding in his opinion, Dundy wrote that no case had ever "appealed so strongly to my sympathy as the one now under consideration." He found the plight of Standing Bear and the Ponca in their suit for a writ of habeas corpus to present the pathetic spectacle of "the remnants of a once numerous and powerful, now weak, insignificant, unlettered and generally despised race" against the might of "the most powerful, most enlightened, and most christianized nations of modern times" (95).

The circumstances of the Ponca flight elicited the most heartfelt sentiment, according to journalist (and later novelist) Thomas Henry Tibbles. Feelings sympathetic to the Ponca ran so high, in Dundy's opinion, that "if the strongest possible sympathy could give the relators title to freedom, they would have been restored to liberty the moment the arguments in their behalf had been closed" (*Standing Bear* 96). But in deciding in favor of Standing Bear and the twenty-five other Ponca prisoners, Dundy based his legal opinion on "the principles of law," which necessarily superseded sentiment: "In a country where liberty is regulated by law, something more satisfactory and enduring than mere sympathy must furnish and constitute the basis of juridical action" (96).[25] Apparently opposing stolid masculine rationality to transitory feminine emotion, this ruling implied a negative principle for anchoring the legal logic of the case in what was *not* obvious. If basing the decision upon sympathy would make the operation of the law seemingly transparent, then Dundy would assert the otherwise invisible principles upon which the "title to freedom" had its basis. The very exercise of the law's power ensured its own invisibility so as to render necessary making visible the principles of its otherwise invisible operation; in adjudicating the lopsided conflict in favor of "this wasted race," the federal legal system proved its ability to disappear as a nationalist expression of power through its apparent ability to adjudicate impartially social conflicts among those subjected to the nation's power (95). In having been granted the writ of habeas corpus, the Ponca appeared to have triumphed in the legal arena over the military force that could surely defeat the tribal nation on the battlefield.

Upon the release of Standing Bear and his followers from military custody, Tibbles, the editor of the *Omaha Daily Herald*, arranged for

Standing Bear to give lectures upon the Eastern seaboard. Lending his credentials as a veteran abolitionist, Wendell Phillips wrote the dedication to Tibbles's account of the Ponca affair. For the nascent Indian reform movement, the outcome of the court case generated by the military's detention of the Ponca went far beyond the immediate release of a small number of Indian individuals. The decision promised a revolutionary transformation of what the Indian reform movement considered as the anomalous relationship between the tribal nations and the federal government.

Attending Standing Bear's talk in Boston in 1879 induced Jackson to become one of the nation's most outspoken advocates for Indian policy reform. Jackson hoped that the Ponca case would establish the legal precedent to "do for the Indian race precisely what the Emancipation act did for the negro" (*Letters* 36). Having the legal personhood of the Indian recognized would be the first, necessary step towards other, even more important legal developments. Just as Emancipation had not only freed the enslaved but had also initiated a long train of legislation to protect the freedmen's freedom in the form of civil rights statutes and constitutional amendments, the *Standing Bear v. Crook* decision signaled to the Indian reform movement the possibility of employing appeals to moral judgment in mustering the political will to destroy tribal sovereignty and to transform the savage without the law into a U.S. citizen.

The heart of the problem for the Indian reform movement was the federal government's seemingly inexplicable insistence upon treating tribes as nations. For the Indian policy reformers, corrupt and despotic Indian agents were ultimately more the effect than the cause of the decline in Indian populations. The reservation system and its incorrigible administration merely followed as the inevitable result of the federal recognition of tribal sovereignty. While treaty making with the tribes had been suspended by Congress in 1871, the legislation did not alter the obligations of the federal government to observe treaties ratified prior to the ban. Henry S. Pancoast, a Philadelphia attorney and a founding organizer of the Indian Rights Association, wrote in his 1884 treatise *The Indian Before the Law* that the relative military and social weakness of the early republic made the Indian tribes' "independent nationality" an incontestable "fact, and its recognition a necessity" (160). By the 1880s, with the relative power of the United States and the tribes reversed, "this treatment of Indian tribes as separate nations" became "the fundamental error in our policy" (160). Now "a fiction and an absurdity," tribal sovereignty prevented the civilized "absorption of the Indian" into the nation as citizens, according to Pancoast: "Just so long as these Indians are alienated by their political independence, so long will they be comparatively impervious to the refining and elevating influence of civilization. Just so long as they are left without the developing and educating restraint and protection of civilized law, so long will they be lawless" (161). Separated from civilization by law yet not governed by it, Indians were driving themselves extinct because the federal government falsely considered the tribes to hold equal national status with the United States itself.

The 1884 U.S. Supreme Court case of *Elk v. Wilkins* further highlighted the complex legal debate over the sovereignty of tribal nations and the status of an individual Indian's civilized state upon nationality. This ruling upheld a Federal District Court's finding that the plaintiff, John Elk, an Indian born in tribal relations but living in Omaha, Nebraska, apart from his tribal nation, was not a citizen of the United States under the terms of the Fourteenth Amendment and therefore not entitled to the franchise. Associate Justice Horace Gray wrote in the Court's majority opinion that

> Indians born within the territorial limits of the United States, members of, and owing immediate allegiance to, or of the Indian tribes (an alien, though dependent power), although in a geographical sense born in the United States, are no more "born in the United States and subject to the jurisdiction thereof," within the meaning of the first section of the Fourteenth Amendment, than the children of subject of any foreign government born within the domain of that government, or the children born within the United States, of ambassadors or other public ministries of foreign nations. (112 U.S. 94)

The Court's majority upheld the legal status of tribal nations as distinct political communities whose sovereignty highlighted the rhetorical basis of U.S. national sovereignty as well. Civilized Indians "born in tribal relations" could not exchange tribal citizenship for U.S. citizenship "at their own will, without the action or assent of the United States" as manifested through treaties or congressional legislation (112 U.S. 94). In other words, both nations had to consent to alter the citizenship status of anyone subject to one national jurisdiction who wished to become subject to another.

If in upholding tribal sovereignty the Supreme Court's majority had to emphasize the consensually dependent nature of the political relationship between the United States and the tribal nations, Associate Justice John Marshall Harlan maintained in his dissent that the majority's stance depended upon what he considered as the fictional equality of tribal nations with the United States. Citing the Marshall court's opinion in *Cherokee Nation v. State of Georgia* that tribal nations' very "state of pupilage" rendered illusional any notion of consensual relations, Harlan opined that the Civil Rights Act of 1866, confirmed and strengthened by the Fourteenth Amendment, rendered any Indian born within U.S. borders who chose "civilization" over tribal relations a U.S. citizen. The fiction of tribal sovereignty held only as long as an Indian chose to remain in tribal relations. In other words, savage (i.e., kinship) nationality was not equivalent to civilized (territorial) nationality. Savage modes of government applied only to savages, Harlan suggested, while civilized government pertained to the civilized. In Harlan's view, the majority's insistence upon the equivalence of savage nationality and U.S. nationality created "a despised and rejected class of persons, with no nationality whatever; who, born in our territory, owing no allegiance to any foreign power, and subject, as residents of the States, to all the burdens of government, are yet not members of any political community nor entitled to any of the rights, privileges, or immunities of citizens of the United States" (112 U.S. 94). For the ex-slaveholder Harlan, the majority's opinion implied that detribalized Indians would have no more rights than free blacks held before Emancipation. Similarly, Indian policy reformers emphasized how rulings such as *Elk v. Wilkins* only emphasized the contradictory and counterproductive legal position that detribalized Indians occupied before U.S. law, while the bastion of savagery itself, the tribal nation, received protective encouragement under the same law. Adopting the tenets of civilization was apparently insufficient to transform an Indian into a U.S. citizen. Indian policy reformers realized that the tribal nations would either have to be acknowledged as conceptually equal with the United States (the understanding that had resulted in the reservation system), or would have to be abolished to enable the true domestication of Indians. Maintaining that tribal sovereignty neither allowed Indians redress through the U.S. courts nor encouraged their entry into civilization, the Indian reform movement made the abolition of tribal sovereignty a key goal.

Ramona and Indian Domestication

To save the Indians from themselves meant promoting the national will to ensure their domestication, a project Jackson would undertake in *Ramo-*

na. Perhaps for this reason Jackson chose to write about the plight of the so-called Mission Indians of Southern California, who had never ascended to the status of nation, or rather had never been recognized by the U.S. government in treaties as such. Even as the artful aesthetics of domestic influence worked to convince citizens to support Indian reform measures, the narrative would construct the Indian as, if not quite yet part of the nation, capable of civilization through a carefully supervised racial tutelage. Unlike Manifest Domesticity, which operated upon the principle of the deportation of freed slaves in the works of Stowe, Jackson thought that racial tutelage through domestic influence could prepare Indians for the ultimate recognition and protection of their title to freedom: U.S. citizenship. Significantly, scientific theories of civilizational development that emerged during the three decades between *Uncle Tom's Cabin* and *Ramona* significantly altered the terms upon which racial reform operated. Whereas Stowe drew heavily from a racial romanticism whose basis for action was the Christian brotherhood of all peoples, Jackson's reformist impulses, although still inflected by Christianity, were fundamentally informed by Darwinian and post-Darwinian anthropology.[26]

In her recourse to the terms "savagery" and "civilization," Jackson invoked the teleological scheme of cultural history propounded by Lewis Henry Morgan, widely credited as the founder of the scientific discipline of anthropology in the United States. Morgan's work on the evolutionary development of civilization emerged as the leading account of colonial difference in the fledgling field of anthropology, elaborated in a series of studies from the 1851 *League of the Iroquois* through the 1879 *Houses and House-life of the American Aborigines*. In these works, Morgan systematically developed a conceptual framework for the colonial management of indigenes in which domesticity figured prominently.[27] In his most influential work, *Ancient Society* (1877), Morgan elaborated a universal developmental trajectory of human culture from the lowest stages of savagery through the middle stages of barbarism to the highest stages of civilization, stages that existed not only historically in sequence for any given human community but also coexisted simultaneously in the present between different cultural groups. Morgan's narrative of civilization identified Aryan civilization, as manifested in European nations and especially the United States, as the apex of cultural development, whereas tribal societies in Africa, Australia, and the Americas generally occupied the more developmentally primitive stages of savagery or barbarism.

Refuting polygenecist accounts of humanity's origins, Morgan posited all races as belonging to the same species but historically developing at different rates along the scale of increasing culture. Cultural differences, in other words, were figured as temporal differences on a single, universal scale. The present-day savage was what the civilized had been centuries or millennia ago. At once a cultural ancestor of the currently civilized and a living cultural fossil, Indians had qualitatively less culture than whites. Guided by the civilized white race, Indians only needed to advance through the developmental stages of culture in order to achieve civilization. Cultural advancement consisted of two main categories. Invention described the contingent technological advancements that allowed humanity to improve the conditions of subsistence through the manufacture of weaponry, pottery, and textiles, the discovery of fire, the cultivation of plants, and the domestication of herd animals. The development of inventions was historical, contingent; progress varied according to the material conditions available to a specific group at any particular time.

In the second category lay the true seeds of culture whose development were teleological and constant: the institutions of family, government, and property. In contrast, the development of institutions invariably followed the same inevitable path of development despite material differences between peoples. Only developmental differences explained the myriad manifestations of these institutions across the world's peoples. The most important institutional developments were those stemming from the sexual division of labor. Morgan's *Ancient Society* traced the relational development of the domestic and the state as the genealogy of separate spheres, relegating women to a pre-political status within civilization and nonwhites to a pre-civilizational status within modernity. What made civilization civilized was the different foundational principle upon which people related to each other.

For Morgan, kinship in pre-civilizational societies determined the entire range of social relationships in savage and barbarian societies. There were no relationships that were not essentially domestic ones, or fictive extensions thereof. In savagery and barbarism, kinship as mediated through the historically variable family form determined the nature of governance. All relationships were personal or personalized kinship ties that determined the structure of not only families but of clans, tribes, and even confederacies of tribes. Specifically, matrilocal kinship determined these relationships. In essence, all relationships, including those of governance, were what in a civilized condition would be classified as domestic relationships. Kinship formed the social universe within which relationships could be imagined. Hence Morgan's fascination with Indian dwellings, which he felt provided the scientific evidence that matriarchal governance in Indian societies was essentially an extension or elaboration of domestic relationships.[28]

In contrast, civilization subsumed the organizational principle of kinship under savagery and barbarism into the vestigial vehicle for the transfer of private property. Relations between people were mediated not by kinship but by property. Kinship had been privatized and removed as the general principle by which relationships were governed as the public sphere of the state arose to guarantee the abstract, independent existence of property. The state generated the archive necessary to track the transfer of property between unrelated individuals, ensconcing the principle of governance on the basis of national territory made up of individual property holdings. Morgan applied the Latin term *societas* to the kinship governance system of pre-civilizational peoples, and the term *civitas* to the property-based national governments of the civilized. The subsumption of *societas*, or the kinship mode of social governance, by *civitas*, or the territorial mode of state rule, was predicated upon the complete removal of women from governance in the new states. Only when women were removed from governance could a state emerge guaranteeing fully elaborated property relations. Within Morgan's evolutionary scheme of culture, both racial and gender hierarchies are reproduced through the inevitable, teleological development of institutions. Patriarchal relations between white women and white men stood as the inevitable, necessary guarantee of racialized difference between the civilized and the primitive, the colonizer and the colonized.

Drawing upon Morgan's theory to categorize the condition of the Mission Indians, Jackson toured the Southern California countryside as a Special Agent to the Commissioner of Indian Affairs for three months in mid-1883. Having received the charge to investigate the Mission Indians as a result of *A Century of Dishonor*, Jackson would base an official report, *Ramona*, and a series of California travelogue sketches for the *Independent* upon her observations. Seeing the properly gendered division of labor in their villages, Jackson found the Mission Indians to have attained a level of civilization above the typical Indian savagery, as indicated by their villages' remarkable resemblance to white communities. In her report, she wrote that many Mission Indian villages were "industrious, peaceable communities," filled with people "cultivating ground, keeping stock, carrying on their own simple manufacture of pottery, mats, baskets, &c.," and generally "making a living" (*Century of Dishonor* 459). In demonstrating such adaptations to "civilization," the Mission Indians had established "rights . . . quite different from and superior to the mere 'occupancy' right of the wild and uncivilized Indian" (*Century of Dishonor* 461).

For Jackson, the Mission Indians had demonstrated the results of a half-century of racial tutelage in the Spanish Missions. Situated upon prime coastal lands from San Diego to Sonoma, the Missions had been founded by the Franciscan Order lead by Father Junipero Serra in a bid to secure the Spanish Crown's hold on its northernmost province, which was sparsely populated by Spanish subjects. From 1769, when the first Mission was established in present-day San Diego, until 1834, the year the Mexican Republic secularized the Missions and disbursed the lands to form the great Californio *ranchos*, the Missions had served as the economic engines of California, wherein Christianized Indians (called neophytes) labored at supplying the material needs of the remote colony. The Missions had long since fallen into ruins by the time Jackson toured Southern California a half-century after secularization, but her travel narrative *Glimpses of Three Coasts* constructed the memory of the allegedly harmonious relations between whites and Indians, in which the former taught the latter the practices of civilization, as the very model of racial tutelage: "The picture of life in one of these missions during their period of prosperity is unique and attractive. The whole place was a hive of industry: trades plying indoors and outdoors; tillers, herders, vintagers by hundreds, going to and fro; children in schools; women spinning . . . " (55). In this favorable characterization of the semi-civilized status of the Mission Indians, Jackson cited the 1852 report of Benjamin Davis Wilson, then sub-agent for Indian affairs, who also attributed the industrious and cooperative behavior of the Mission Indians to the racial tutelage of the Missions. In comparing the Missions to "a Manchester or Lowell, on a small scale," Wilson's report makes evident how the discipline of supervised labor formed properly ordered regimes of racial and gendered relations (48). "Devoted neither to war or to the chase," "friendly to whites," and on the whole "docile and tractable, and accustomed to subjection," the Mission Indians exhibited "the traits which are always looked to as the grounds of civilization" formed through the labor disciplines instituted by the Franciscans (32). Secularization had all too soon curtailed the racial tutelage of the Missions. In a sentiment echoed by Jackson, Wilson wrote, "In the fall of the Missions . . . philanthropy laments the failure of one of the grandest experiments ever made for the elevation of this unfortunate race" (3).

But labor discipline in and of itself seemed insufficient to complete the civilizing project left unfinished. If the Missions and their institutional successors, the short-lived farm reservations of the 1850s, could not be revived in the 1880s, then Jackson and the Indian reform movement would inculcate the desire for civilization among the Indians through domestic influence. In her report on the Mission Indians, Jackson advocated the expanded presence of female educators, whose civilizing touch would reach far beyond the classroom into the Indian home: "Women have more courage and self-denying missionary spirit . . . and have an invaluable influence outside their school-rooms. They go familiarly into the homes, and are really educating the parents as well as the children in a way which is not within the power of any man, however earnest and devoted he may be" (*Century of Dishonor* 469). Having taught the freedmen the lessons of democracy, white women could similarly lift the Indians into civilization. Educating Indian women in the arts of domestic influence would bring Indian men into the pale of civilization once the work of white women was done. Secretary of the Interior Schurz commented, "Nothing will be more apt to raise the Indians in the scale of civilization than to stimulate their attachment of permanent homes, and it is woman that must make the atmosphere and form the attraction of the home. She must be recognized, with affection and respect, as the center of domestic life" (16).

In *Ramona*, the protagonist's own domestic influence can turn "a wretched place" of a mud hut into a sliver of civilization (337). Aunt Ri, the peripatetic Southerner whose own "affectionate disorderly genius" seems less developed in this direction, exclaims, "It beats all ever I see, the way thet Injun woman's got fixed up out er nothin" (337–38). Making civilization out of savagery via this display of orderly domesticity, Ramona transforms a room of "the mud hovel" into "jest like a parlor!" (337). Most importantly for the reformers, Indian children would come under the all-important domestic influences of their mothers, thus suggesting to Schurz an attractive and cost-effective way of making the Indian disappear: "If we educate the girls of to-day, we educate the mothers of to-morrow, and in educating those mothers we prepare the ground for the education of generations to come" (16). Through their domestic housework, opined Indian Agent Wilson, Indian women "may be among the most efficient civilizers" (50).

Tying Indian men to the land, Indian women formed the essential link between the need to labor and the desire for private property. Domesticity thus articulated the essential conditions for destroying tribal sovereignty and thus savagery itself. Bound by the invisible but pervasive influence of domestic interiors, Indian men would find the necessary impetus to leave tribal communalism for wage labor. President of Amherst College Merrill Edward Gates, a prominent member of the Lake Mohonk Conference of the Friends of the Indian, defined the civilizing link between labor and the desire for private property as the essential difference between the savage Indian and the civilized American:

> We have, to begin with, the absolute need of awakening in the savage Indian broader desires and ampler wants. To bring him out of savagery into citizenship we must make the Indian more intelligently selfish before we can make him unselfishly intelligent. We need to *awaken in him wants*. In his dull savagery he must be touched by the wings of the divine angel of discontent. Then he begins to look forward, to reach out. The desire for property of his own may become an intense educating force. The wish for a home of his own awakens him to new efforts. Discontent with the teepee and the starving rations of the Indian camp in winter is needed to get the Indian out of the blanket and into trousers,—and trousers with a pocket in them, and with a *pocket that aches to be filled with dollars!* (334; emphasis in original)

Wage labor is then the effect of the domestic desire for property, which itself indicates the conversion of the savage, communal Indian into the "intelligently selfish," autonomous, rational actor of classic laissez-faire economics. Only as this economic subject could the Indian then enter into the social contract of the "intelligently unselfish" nation. In fulfilling the desire for property, the racial tutelage of wage labor would make the Indian vanish, leaving instead the citizen.

The Limits of Reform

The project of racial tutelage, while essential for transforming the Indian into the citizen, nonetheless had its limits and hazards. According to Jackson, the supersession of tribal habits and relations could potentially take many years of concerted effort upon the part of whites: "It is strange how sure civilized peoples are, when planning and legislating for savages, to forget that it has always taken centuries to graft on or evolve out of savagery anything like civilization" (*Glimpses* 60). The danger of being overly optimistic was one the U.S. government could learn from the annals of previous Spanish colonial Indian policy: "With singular lack of realization of the time needed to make citizens out of savages," the Spanish crown had considered a decade sufficient time to inculcate upon the neophytes the tenets of Christian civilization. For Jackson, "five times ten years would have been little enough to allow for getting such a scheme fairly underway, and another five times ten years for the finishing and rounding of the work" (60).

But even if the long apprenticeship in civilization was taken into account, there remained the disturbing possibility that the Indians, even those ready to become individual property owners like Alessandro Assis of *Ramona*, might still never fully retain the lessons of racial tutelage. At first glance, Alessandro embodies the living legacy of the Mission's civilizing influence. The son of the "right-hand man" to the Franciscan priest at Mission San Luis Rey, the literate Alessandro is not only a skilled sheep shearer but also a talented vocalist and musician whose sweet strains help bring the Californio ranchero Felipe Moreno back to life after a severe illness.

But other invisible yet equally powerful influences could exert themselves through the layered veneer of civilization. Civilized example might be superior to civilized precept, yet neither were certain to overcome still earlier lessons in savagery engraved within the body. Perhaps the most widely accepted theory of biological inheritance before the rediscovery of Mendelian genetics at the turn of the century, the neo-Lamarckian transmission of acquired characteristics ensured that what culture developed the body would remember. Just as the neo-Lamarckian mechanism of the inheritance of acquired characteristics allowed acquired or invented culture to be readily translated into biological race, the atavistic retentions of the latter could erupt into the lives of even the fully civilized. For Morgan, racial reversion explained some of what he considered as deviant social phenomena within modern civilization:

> In the light of these facts some of the excrescences of modern civilization, such as Mormonism, are seen to be relics of the old savagism not yet eradicated from the human brain. We have the same brain, perpetuated by reproduction, which worked in the skulls of barbarians and savages in by-gone ages; and it has come down to us ladened and saturated with the thoughts aspirations and passions, with which it was busied through the intermediate periods. . . . These outcrops of barbarism are so many revelations of its ancient proclivities. They are explainable as a species of mental atavism. (61)

That barbaric atavisms such as Mormonism flourished out West, where the institutions of civilization were weakest, was no coincidence.

Indeed, white women often found that even white men needed to be domesticated out on the frontier. In the absence of church or government, only the home countered white men's proclivity for civilizational backsliding. Discourses of middle-class domesticity worked to reverse the unsavory or violent aspects of masculinist imperialist adventuring all too often brought home. What in the discourse of imperialist adventuring signified a redemptive opportunity to regain manhood became in the discourse of Indian policy reform the embarrassing collapsing of difference between the civilized and the primitive. In her 1868 essay "An Appeal for the Indians," Lydia Maria Child denounced how U.S. military campaigns against tribal nations became nothing more than a catalogue of war crimes. For Child, report after report of massacres of Indians committed by U.S. soldiers begged the very question of civilization itself: "But are we civilized? When I reflect upon what we *have* done, and *are* doing toward our red brethren, I cannot in conscience answer yes" (87). The masculinized violence of frontline imperialism especially endangered the civilized status of white men. Reverting to barbaric warfare, white men only demoted themselves to the cultural level of their primitive enemies, casting the very basis of colonial difference in doubt.

When racial reversion affected white men, white women would provide the guidance to recall the moral lessons of domestic influence. After Aunt Ri chides young Merrill for his callous support of villainous settler Jim Farrar in Alessandro's death, he finds himself shaken to the very moral core:

> Aunt Ri's earnest words . . . reached a depth in his nature which had been long untouched; a stratum, so to speak, which lay far beneath the surface. The character of the Western frontiersman is often a singular accumulation of such strata,—the training and beliefs of his earliest days overlain by succession of unrelated and violent experiences, like geological deposits. Underneath the exterior crust of the most hardened and ruffianly nature often remains—its forms not yet quite fossilized—a realm full of the devout customs, doctrines, religious influences, which the boy knew, and the man remembers. By sudden upheaval, in some great catastrophe or struggle in his mature life, these all come again into the light. (406–7)

Hidden but not forgotten, early domestic training could influence adult moral judgment and contest the demoralizing experiences of the harsh frontier environment.[29] But if Californian Merrill finds that he is really "New Englander yet at heart," the ever-precarious racial fault lines of California reveal Alessandro as always an Indian savage rather than a potential citizen (407).[30]

Brooding upon the "the wrongs he had borne, the hopeless outlook for his people in the future, and most of all on the probable destitution and suffering in store for Ramona," Alessandro's "brain gave way" to hurts "gone too deep." "Secretly brooding upon the wrongs he had borne" cracks "his self-contained, reticent, repressed nature" and allows the unconscious savage to surface (366). Mentally unstable, Alessandro drifts into intervals of delusions "always shaped by the bitterest experience of his life"; recovering, he "had no recollection of what had happened" (367). One such spell becomes Alessandro's death at the hands of Farrar: Alessandro inadvertently takes Farrar's horse during such an amnesiac episode. Before his death Alessandro attributed his madness to having chosen an individual fate over communal existence. Returning from seeing his people driven from Temecula, he tells Ramona, "It is the saints who have punished me thus for having resolved to leave my people, and take all I had for myself and you" (206).

But the text belies this self-explication of the malady, suggesting rather that Alessandro suffers from never really having left his tribal nation at all. Farrar's casual shooting of Alessandro depends not only upon a legal system that barred Indians from testifying against whites, but also upon Farrar's privileges of whiteness that enable him to execute acts of punishment for property crimes. Leaving Alessandro to die, he shouts, "That'll teach you damned Indians to leave off stealing our horses!" (371). But if Farrar's attribution of criminal intent to Alessandro speaks more of the racist construction of all Indians as inherently criminal, then precisely the lack of criminal intent on Alessandro's part also indicates his distance from understandings of private property. Indian policy reformer Pancoast noted that "the Indians among themselves are wonderfully free from the crimes which infest civilization," particularly property crimes, but "strangely as it may sound, it must be remembered that these crimes are to some extent the unfortunate incidents and creatures of a higher states of social development." The general recognition of "the right of individual property" was "indispensable to robbery"; "inseparable from our civilization," property crimes indexed the degree to which any civilization had truly progressed (163). In other words, property crimes represented an improper relationship to actual property but the correct conceptual relationship to, and recognition of, private property.

Alessandro may have never intended to steal the horse, but criminal intent would have precisely indicated his recognition of the horse *as* private property. Rather, his misrecognition of the horse *not* as private property resulted from his *not* recognizing any private property whatsoever. Alessandro's madness is thus characterized precisely by a misrecognition of the status of livestock as private property. In such a delusional state he would often "enter any enclosure he saw, where there were sheep or cattle, go about among them, speaking of them to passers-by as his own" (367). This imaginary appropriation is less a personal enrichment than an elemental repetition of the now-lost tribal wealth his father had held as a communal trust. Despite keeping nearly as many sheep as the Morenos themselves, Pablo Assis remains poor rather than wealthy because he "feeds and supports half his village" (92). Before the tribe's eviction from Temecula, Alessandro was to have succeeded his father as caretaker of his band's communal resources. Alessandro's madness, in effect, is presented as an atavistic reversion to a state of savagery that does not recognize private property. Civilization could take the Indian out of the tribal nation, but not the tribal nation out of the Indian.

While Aunt Ri vocalizes Jackson's outrage at Alessandro's murder, the episode nonetheless highlights the fragile nature of racial tutelage and the perceived danger of racial reversions. As the project of civilizing the savage is cast into doubt, the possibility of incorporating the Indian into the nation as a citizen recedes for the text. Rather, racial reversions make clear the impossibility of making the Indian disappear into U.S. citizenship. If Ramona herself remains, deep down, a semi-barbaric Californiana rather than a savage Indian, nevertheless the danger of racial reversion is always present in her mestiza blood. Both she and Felipe, with his heartfelt desire to marry and misceginate, must leave the United States for Mexico in order to keep the nation white and free from the invisible, insidious influence of mixed blood. In essence, the attempt in *Ramona* to incorporate Indians into the nation is thus less about making Indians disappear into citizenship as it is about ensuring the hegemony of liberal deployments of colonial difference.

Insofar as the romantic union of Alessandro and Ramona ends in his death and her removal to Mexico as Felipe's bride, the failed national allegory of *Ramona* suggests precisely the impossibility of incorporating indigenous people within the post-Reconstruction national imaginary. Arguably, Ramona and Felipe's exile to Mexico is the trace of Manifest Domesticity's earlier function to ensure national whiteness through expulsion of nonwhite populations. Jackson not only ensures that miscegenation never occurs domestically but also rhetorically banishes questions of racial injustices (such as the Californios' dispossession and the hyperexploitation of mestizos and Indians) from the national political agenda. Jackson's national allegory disseminated the possibilities of seeing the Indian as an American rather than as an Indian in the liberal choice to domesticate rather than exterminate, thus allowing the possibility that the citizen could replace the savage through the powerful but invisible effects of domestic influence. By making widely available the possibility of making the Indian vanish through the unconscious influence of racial tutelage, this liberal narrative of colonial difference also insured that the unconscious influence of race would foreclose any successful attempts at Indian domestication. Hidden in the blood, the racial reversions of *Ramona* reveal the national allegory as a representational strategy for managing colonial difference, making available new ways of constructing the Indian as disenfranchised, deterritorialized wage labor rather than as an obstacle to national economic development.

White Feminism and Empire

Liberal imperialism confounds rigid notions of colonial rule in offering national inclusion to the colonized, promising ultimate convergence into the colonizer's civil society. Deployments of colonial mimicry depend upon the imagined transformations of the colonizer/colonized relationship promised by colonial education of the natives. Ultimately, the colonial fantasy is that the colonizers, exercising their moral duty to bring civilization to dark hinterlands, are there for the good of the colonized. At once reassuring morals and pocketbooks, colonial mimicry ensures that the material exploitation of native labor and resources proceeds in all good conscience. Insofar as civilization is synonymous with whiteness in the late nineteenth century, colonial rule both depends upon, and deplores, the necessarily shifty, shiftless, and shifting borders of civilization. Basing the future abolition of colonial difference on a colonial mimicry founded upon theories of cultural development creates the very disciplinary management of "race" itself *as* the border of the United States. Thus national allegory, far from incorporating racial Others, becomes the hegemonic representational technology for keeping the nation white.

In the late nineteenth century, the liberal reconceptualization of colonial difference ultimately reaffirmed colonial relationships while further normalizing the role of white women within the state's management of racial hierarchies. If the teleology of civilizational development depended upon the emergence of a gendered public/domestic dichotomy, then transformed U.S. colonial policies of benevolent assimilation generated new regimes of gendered power relations that allowed white women to become more fully enabled social actors through colonial practices. White women's participation in nineteenth-century social reform movements (particularly abolition and Indian policy reform) not only resulted in what they considered as steps towards the relative normalization of state functioning in relationship to slaves or Indians but also in relation to themselves.[31] Hence, the moral imperative of the domesticity-influenced reform novel to address federal policies not only concerned the morality of such practices but also introduced new modes of direct participation for white women within the colonial project. By representing the domestic influence of white women as the necessary mediation needed to civilize Indians and consequently bring them under U.S. law, the Indian reform novel made possible the later deployment of white women as state agents of colonial policy.

The reformers' belief in the uplifting domestic influence of white women became institutionalized through a government program implemented at the behest of the Women's National Indian Association by the early 1890s. The field matron program sent white women onto reservations for the express purpose of inculcating the sexual division of labor of "the spheres." Just as farmers and mechanics provided Indian men with the example of manly labor, field matrons would provide Indian women with the example of proper domesticity.[32] Likewise, white women were employed by the federal government as teachers upon reservations and at the Indian boarding schools, whereas before the Civil War the regular and widespread public or governmental employment of white women (even if unmarried) in any context remained relatively rare.[33] Whereas mid-century modes of domesticity had typically emphasized moral reformation of the public sphere through indirect influence, new anthropological theories of civilization made it possible for white women to participate directly within the processes of colonization as U.S. state agents without compromising the moral purity of the domestic sphere. Despite initial opposition to these roles, they would later be elaborated and expanded as part of the U.S. occupation of the Philippines, Guam, and Puerto Rico after the U.S.-Spanish War.[34]

Rather than affix responsibility for U.S. imperialism, the point here is to analyze the hegemonic relations that allowed the discourse of domesticity to present as emancipatory (both for white women and the objects of their reform activities) yet another set of colonial practices. To the extent that the Indian reform movement made the formal normalization of Indians as U.S. citizens synonymous with and contingent upon the civilizational difference of colonial mimicry, the domestic terms of national incorporation ensure that state functioning would forge a politically, economically, and culturally subordinated position for individual Indians within the nation while simultaneously dismantling tribal nations.[35] By removing the work of national integration out of the conflictual public sphere of political power and into the apparently non-coercive (but not apolitical) domestic space of the home and family, the Indian reform novel occluded the agency of those who might not wish to represent the colorful counterpoint to the warp of whiteness. In the long run, reform policies only succeeded in further marginalizing and dispossessing Indians.[36] As a discourse of colonial mimicry, the domestication of Indians sought national integration by collapsing cultural differences through education while assuring that racial difference would always serve as a ready marker of the impossibility of that task. The ambivalence of colonial mimicry, as Bhabha has pointed out, is that the continual deferral of colonial difference makes apparent the contradictions of the discourse, hence delegitimizing colonial authority even as it is asserted.[37] The legacy of this policy of colonial mimicry is the mimic citizen, both beloved and despised, celebrated but feared, enfranchised yet powerless. Liberal projects based upon hierarchies of culture repeat colonial difference under emancipatory guise, always deferring the question of full citizenship rights for people of color.

CHAPTER 4

Blushing Brides and Soulless Corporations

Racial Formation in
María Amparo Ruiz de Burton's
The Squatter and the Don

Helen Hunt Jackson's 1884 novel *Ramona* and María Amparo Ruiz de Burton's 1885 novel *The Squatter and the Don* are practically literary twins in their common representation of late nineteenth-century social relations in Southern California. Both novels depict the complex interactions and frequent conflicts between Californio rancheros, displaced Indians, and white settlers. Published just a year apart, and with the same general cast of characters and the same palpable concern with the place of racial difference within the nation, these novels have sometimes been paired in critical studies. These novels are seen alternatively as criticizing U.S. representational regimes that perniciously racialized Californios and Indians or as invidiously constituting those very practices.[1] Both participate in shifting post-Reconstruction nation building away from the divisive problem of North and South in the aftermath of slavery to the differently racialized issues of tribal sovereignty and Mexican American civil rights. As discussed in the previous chapter, the domestic aesthetics of the Indian reform movement imagined a united imperial nation through the domesticating project of civilizing savage Indians and semi-barbaric Mexicans out West.

The colonial difference between Indians and whites in *Ramona* is articulated through a reformist discourse of civilization that transformed the pseudo-biological paradigm of absolute racial difference into a temporalculturalist paradigm of relative racial difference. Within this latter paradigm, the Californios of *Ramona* in some ways embody Jackson's model of tolerant inclusivity for the United States in their apparently harmonious relations with Indians. Yet the very dependence of the rancheros upon Indian labor, however sympathetically portrayed, also demonstrated the dangers of cultural and racial degeneration brought about by such intimate contact. In *Glimpses of Three Coasts*, Jackson implied that the natural fecundity of California explained "the character, or, to speak more accurately, the lack of character, of the old Mexican and Spanish Californians" (28). Challenged neither intellectually nor physically by the need to make the land productive, the mestizo descendants of the Spanish conquistadors had degenerated into "merry people of Mexican and Spanish blood, [who troubled] themselves about nothing, dancing away whole days and nights like children" (56). Even the most enlightened Californios scarcely showed aptitude for either industry or learning. Visiting the family of Don Antonio Coronel in Los Angeles, Jackson noted that the dusty library of the "foremost representatives of ideas and progress in the City of Angels" revealed that "the old atlases, primers, catechisms, grammars, reading-books . . . meant toil and trouble to the merry, ignorant children of the merry and ignorant people" of Alta California (121).

Jackson did acknowledge that Spanish and Mexican land grants in California protected Indian rights of occupancy, something U.S. law did not. In *Ramona*, the Señora Moreno rightly hurls invectives against the "Yankee" government that "took away from the Señora the greater part of her best pasture-lands" and hence displaced long-standing Indian communities (15). Yet the narrative imputes a characteristic carelessness to the process by which Spanish and Mexican land grants had been parceled: "It might be asked, perhaps, just how General Moreno owned all this land, and the question might not be easy to answer. It was not and could not be answered to the satisfaction of the United States Land Commission, which, after the surrender of California, undertook to sift and adjust Mexican land titles" (15). Racially linked to the very Indians they conscripted into labor, lazy and character-less Californios were similarly infantilized by the anthropological discourse of civilization.

If in Jackson's account the Californios partly had themselves to blame for the loss of their lands after 1848, Ruiz de Burton would provide an alternative reading of California's history centered upon an different account of racial hierarchies and the national families made possible by such an account. *The Squatter and the Don* complicates received notions about how resistance may inhere in texts simply because of perceived racial alterity. Certainly, the layered history of Spanish, Mexican, and U.S. colonialisms complicates any simplistic account of colonial difference in nineteenth-century California.[2] While narratives written by foreign travelers to Alta California before 1848 had invidiously constructed the Californios as degenerate half-breeds, the Californios clearly distinguished themselves from mestizo and Indian workers upon the basis of their purportedly pure Spanish racial heritage and cultural background.[3] As one Californio response to the discourse of Californio degeneracy, *The Squatter and the Don* negotiates multiple layers of colonial histories; the historical contingency of colonial difference in the making of social identities comes to the fore.[4] Such complexities force a reconsideration of the meaning of race itself in such a context. In particular, race can neither be understood as simply binaristic in its deployments within the novel (white/nonwhite, white/black) nor reduced to an interpretive shorthand for indicating specifically oppositional practices. Simultaneously, these complications can neither be interpreted automatically under the sign of resistance nor dismissed as irrelevant to U.S. imperial nation building.

Ruiz de Burton challenges the racial hierarchies that had enabled and legitimated the Anglo dispossession of the Californios, highlighting how the U.S. legal system presumed colonial difference as the basis of its operation. Yet Ruiz de Burton's intervention itself is enmeshed within a Spanish/Mexican colonial logic that would reclaim the very whiteness denied to Californios. *The Squatter and the Don* reconstitutes whiteness as the operative condition of social agency, and hence reifies Californios as "white" even as it erases the preconditions for such claims: the Spanish colonial regime of racialized Indian labor. The novel outlines the inadequacies of what Lora Romero has criticized as "radical alterity," or the structuralist, ahistorical conception of "resistance" as existing prior to and outside of the operation of power (73). So ahistorically situated within literary studies, texts produced by Californios are sometimes assumed to embody pure resistance, and, as a consequence, interpretation becomes an exercise in correctly identifying that resistance.[5] However, if resistance is produced through and within relations of power rather than "outside" those relations, then a critical understanding of historical alterity can begin to address the multiple, and often contradictory, zones of resistance potentially present in any text. As Romero comments, "Resistance may not transcend power relations altogether, but that does not mean that it merely reproduces the same power relations or that all power relations must reproduce the status quo" (87). Ruiz de Burton's intervention in *The Squatter and the Don* indeed generates certain kinds of narrative resistance to racial, gender, and class domination, but not as the pure oppositionality of radical alterity. Rather, this novel's historical alterity outlines precisely the limitations and inadequacies of appropriating national allegory for interpretive projects of dismantling colonial difference.

A Failing National Allegory

In making families, the historical romance makes nations. *The Squatter and the Don* stages the making of a national identity as the inevitability of family ties, ties that organized as a common sense would legitimate the nation as the natural mode for organizing and representing "We the People" over and against other communal practices. As such, the romance of reunion can be recognized generally as the narration of national hegemony itself, and specifically as the establishment of racial difference within the post-Reconstruction intertwining of race and nation.[6] However, in *The Squatter and the Don* the romantic dream of national unity is dispelled by another allegory that ominously promises not the nationalized coupling of families but the disappearance of family and nation altogether. Towards the end of the narrative, the patrician son of a once-wealthy Californio land owner is forced by declining family fortunes to accept "the pitiful wages of a poor hod carrier." Working to build the mansions of San Francisco's newly minted Gilded Age "railroad millionaires," the stoic Gabriel Alamar "never complained," comments the novel's narrator, but "the eloquence of facts had said all that was to be said": "In that hod full of bricks not only his own sad experience was represented, but *the entire history* of the native Californians *of Spanish descent* was epitomized. Yes, Gabriel carrying his hod full of bricks up a steep ladder, was the symbolic representation of his race. The natives, of Spanish origin, having lost all their property, must henceforth be hod carriers" (351; emphasis in original). Rosaura Sánchez and Beatrice Pita have identified this historical trajectory of the Californios as one of a "change in class status, from upper-class to working-class" in Gabriel's transformation "from 'Don' to 'hod carrier.'" This downward mobility, literalized in Gabriel's life-threatening fall in which the very bricks he carries bury him, "constitutes the central resentment at work in the novel" (34). As in national allegory, an individual character represents a specific group or class; but rather than making citizens of the nation, what gets produced through the allegory of proletarianization are racially marked laborers, noncitizens because they are nonwhite. Far from ensuring the integration of Californios into the nation as part of the hegemonic elite, national allegory can no longer provide stable registers of racial and class hierarchies that would ensure the familial production of fraternal citizens. No longer considered white even in a cursory manner by 1885, Californios could not attain the social agency necessary to secure national membership. Despite the multiple marriages between Californio and Anglo elite families that punctuate the novel, the project of national allegory remains radically unrealized.

Hence the decline of the Californios as a landed elite by the 1880s signified not just demotion into the ranks of wage laborers but also the loss of the privileges of whiteness maintained under previous negotiations of national hegemony. Proletarianization is thus not the only cause of resentment at work in this novel, or rather not the only way this resentment is articulated. This change in class status is linked to a change in racialization, so that a proud white genealogy of "Spanish descent" becomes transformed into the demeaning experience of laboring for a transnational corporation under the racial marker of colonial difference. The index of this fall in class status is precisely how wage labor transforms Gabriel from a *criollo* into a California Indian: "The fact that Gabriel was a *native Spaniard*, [his wife Lizzie Mechlin Alamar] saw plainly, militated against them. If he had been rich, his nationality could have been forgiven, but no one will willingly tolerate a *poor native Californian*" (351; emphasis in original). Even the fact of fair complexion, which makes Gabriel and his brother Victoriano "look like Englishmen," is insufficient to arrest Gabriel's social refiguration as a California native, or, in other words, as a California Indian (89). In essence, experiencing downward class mobility as the process of being racialized as nonwhite, the Californios in *The Squatter and the Don* demonstrate the shifting historical registers of social agency during the transformation of Spanish-colonial racial hierarchies into those of the post-Reconstruction United States.

Before the U.S. conquest in 1848, Californio rancheros had often kidnapped Indians from rancherías and forced them to work as ranch hands. The extent to which the rancheros depended upon indentured Indian labor in the period between the secularization of the Franciscan Missions in 1834 until the demise of the rancho economy in the 1870s can be gathered from prominent ranchero Salvador Vallejo's nostalgic comments about Indian laborers during that period:

> Our friendly Indians were missed very much, for they tilled our soil, pastured our cattle, sheared our sheep, cut our lumber, built our houses, paddled our boats, made tiles for our houses, ground our grain, killed our cattle and dress their hides for market, and made our burnt bricks, while the Indian women made excellent servants, took good care of our children, made every one of our meals, and be it said in justice to them that, though not learned in the culinary arts as taught by Italian and French books, they made very palatable and savory dishes. (qtd. in Sánchez, *Telling Identities* 172)

Little changed after the U.S. conquest in this colonial labor regime. Guaranteed U.S. citizenship by the Treaty of Guadalupe Hidalgo, the rancheros helped block citizenship status for Indians at the California state constitutional convention. Working to retain a large pool of disenfranchised laborers, Californios subsequently influenced the passage of laws that guaranteed a cheap, vulnerable labor force when labor shortages hampered their ability to profit from the boom in cattle prices brought about by the Gold Rush. Taking over Californio labor practices as well as Californio land, Anglo settlers readily joined the rancheros in legally codifying the long-standing Californio labor practice of Indian servitude, thus availing themselves of a legalized form of bondage in a free labor state.[7] In a rehearsal of the post-Reconstruction South's notorious convict lease system, vagrancy laws such as the so-called 1855 "Greaser Act" allowed for the lease of offenders (usually indigent Indians or mestizos) for a specified time as cheap, no-wage labor granted only room and board. Similarly, the Indenture Act of 1850 allowed for the involuntary bonding of Indians to a U.S. citizen for at least a decade with no remuneration.[8]

While the few appearances of Indian servants in *The Squatter and the Don* serve mainly as opportunities for the Alamars to complain about Indian "laziness," the general invisibility of Indian labor in the narrative belies the degree to which the wealth they produced also manufactured Californio "whiteness" before and after 1848.[9] Certainly the Spanish colonial racial hierarchy, largely maintained during the Mexican period, had emphasized *limpieza de sangre* (purity of blood), despite this gesture's easy effacement of the Californios' historically mestizo origins. In danger of losing their dominant status as white after the U.S. conquest, the Californios traded upon their status as class elites in post-1848 California to construct an Anglo-Californio hegemony that at some fundamental level granted them rights and privileges as white citizens, and these political concessions resulted in real material advantages from the resulting increased control of Indian labor. Ultimately, as the example of Gabriel Alamar demonstrates, in the post-Reconstruction national ordering of racial hierarchy the only begrudged difference between an Indian daylaborer and a "Spanish" Don was indeed the whiteness that Indian labor on Californio ranchos had created. Precisely this renewed figuration of whiteness is what *The Squatter and Don* attempts to renegotiate for the Californios in the years following Reconstruction as they collectively experienced proletarianization. Deploying an affective national allegory encoded not simply in fair complexions but in blushing subjectivities, the narrative seeks to restore a lost social agency for the Californios within the bodily signification of whiteness.

Yet as a "poor native Californian," Gabriel Alamar also stands not as a (white) citizen of the United States but as the indigenous colonized of the novel's railroad empires, "the Napoleons of this land whose power the sons of California can neither check, nor thwart, nor escape, nor withstand" (365). If *The Squatter and the Don* works to enact a class-based, bodily representational technology of whiteness within constructions of U.S. nationalism, then the ruins of this project trace the historical trajectory of the Californios' corporate dispossession by indicating how national allegory could no longer translate the affective parameters of race into privileged positions within a national hierarchy by the 1880s. Rather than (re)mapping the blushing white body of the nineteenth-century historical romance as the privileged indicator of the nation's racialized parameters of social agency, *The Squatter and the Don* exhibits the disarticulation of the sympathetic white body from the national interpretive frame that empowered it. A monopolistic corporate hermeneutics is articulated, with the prosthetics of empire superceding racial categories, and transnational networks of corporate capital exceeding national limits. Unable to celebrate nationally (re)productive unions, *The Squatter and the Don* foregrounds the inability of national allegory to reestablish the racialized terms of national unity in the face of social relations restructured by emergent transnational corporations.

Wedding Whiteness

Born in 1833, María Amparo Ruiz de Burton came from a prominent family with significant land holdings in the sparsely populated northern Mexican province of Baja California. During the U.S. invasion of Baja California during the U.S.-Mexican War, Ruiz de Burton met and married U.S. Army Captain Henry S. Burton, the field commander of the U.S. forces in the area. Subsequently moving to the new U.S. territory of California, first to Monterrey and then to San Diego, the Burtons purchased Rancho Jamul in San Diego County. This property would figure prominently in Ruiz de Burton's life, even if the Burtons and their two children spent many years on the East Coast in Virginia, Delaware, New York, Rhode Island, and Washington, DC. Cosmopolitan and well connected, the Burtons moved easily among Eastern elites, participating in events such as President Lincoln's inaugural ball and socializing with Mary Todd Lincoln.[10]

Well educated in Spanish and English literature, Ruiz de Burton published two novels and a comic adaptation of Miguel de Cervantes's *Don Quixote*. Offering a biting satiric critique of U.S. institutional behavior, from the politics of the U.S. Army and the president's office to the domestic mores of genteel New England womanhood, her 1872 novel *Who Would Have Thought It?* counterpoised the hypocritical foibles of a smug, self-congratulatory Eastern establishment with the true romance between the honorable New England lad Julian Norval and the cultured Mexican beauty Lola Medina. Rescued as a youth by Norval's father from hostile Indians in the Southwest who had kidnapped her mother, Lola joins Julian to form a partnership of true elites that unites the nation across cultural and wartime divides. This union becomes possible as the dark dye applied to Lola's white skin by the Indians wears off, allowing Julian and the other Easterners to appreciate Lola for the cultured "Spanish" woman she really is. Freed of the specter of miscegenation, Julian and Lola can proceed to found a new national unity through their union. As José Aranda, Jr. notes, Lola and Julian's marriage represents "a union of two colonial enterprises . . . where Mexican colonialism and its material wealth are merged with U.S. colonialism and its promises of representative democracy" ("Contradictory Impulses" 569).

Yet by the time of the 1885 publication of *The Squatter and the Don*, the prospect of Californios and Anglos jointly managing the grand imperial project of the United States had vanished. Sensing that just one Californio-Anglo romance would no longer suffice, Ruiz de Burton would multiply the romance plots between white Easterners and Californios in *The Squatter and the Don* to no avail. Rather than successfully uniting the elites of the two coasts, this narrative registers the singular impossibility of doing so in the face of changed racial and economic parameters of social agency.

The romantic plot of the novel focuses on the often vexed relationship between the Darrell and Alamar families in Southern California during the latter years of Reconstruction. William Darrell, the white squatter of the title, has encroached upon the lands of Don Mariano Alamar, the patrician Californio ranchero whose livelihood has been threatened by squatter encroachments and legal challenges to his 47,000-acre San Diego County land grant from the Spanish Crown. In order to avoid strife, Darrell's wife Mary tells their son Clarence to purchase 640 acres outright from Don Mariano. In the process Clarence and Don Mariano's daughter Mercedes meet and fall in love.[11] The union of the two families promises to secure the fortunes and futures of both through the affective ties of marriage, but the narrative tells more a tale of familial woe than marital bliss.

Despite the mutual acceptance of Anglo and Californio families (as shown by multiple marriages throughout the narrative between the Alamars and their neighbors, the Mechlins and the Darrells), the Alamars lose their rancho, for which the narrative blames the depredations of squatter hordes, the U.S. government, and the rapacious Central and Southern Pacific Railroads. Yet if monopoly railroad corporations prove most culpable in this eventual decline of the Californios, the betrayals of the U.S. government in adjudicating the property rights of its Californio citizens reveal the invidious distinction made between Anglo and Californio in the latter's dispossession by due process of law. As such, Ruiz de Burton retraces the largely untold history of the Californios' dispossession, a collective history based on the disparate legal treatment of Californio citizens to the material advantage of white ones.

Countering the widespread notion of Californio indolence expressed in Jackson's *Glimpses of Three Coasts*, Ruiz de Burton opens *The Squatter and the Don* with a recapitulation of Californio land dispossession since the signing of the Treaty of Guadalupe Hidalgo in 1848. Decrying federal and state laws that "drive to the wall all owners of cattle ranchos," Don Mariano Alamar reflects how "there are some enactments so obviously intended to favor one class of citizens against another class, that to call them laws is an insult to law" (66). Rather than upholding the rule of law, U.S. law promotes squatter lawlessness against Californio property owners by statutes that "seem more intended to help the law-breakers than to protect the law-abiding" (65). Equating the land loss of the Californios with the failure of the nation to recognize the civil rights of its new Californio citizens, the novel launches a scathing critique of the racialized legal constructions that enabled this dispossession by due process. Ruiz de

Burton exposes the otherwise seamless conventions of the fictional narrative and reveals novelistic discourse as the ideological contestation of nationalist history.

As the novel indicates, the pattern of land dispossession at the heart of the Californio experience of proletarianization varied widely, but generally Californio land holdings in northern California came under squatter pressure as soon as the northern Sierra Nevada gold mines had been largely depleted by the early 1850s. The travels of William Darrell trace the historical progression of squatter encroachments upon Californio holdings across the state. Having "crossed the plains in '48" with the novel's other squatters as his teamsters, Darrell squatted on Californio lands in Sonoma and Napa Counties along with a great number of disappointed gold seekers (64).[12] Unsuccessful in his bid for northern Californio land, Darrell decides at the novel's opening to migrate to San Diego County, where a much smaller influx of Anglo immigrants lessened the possibility that Californio holdings in the southern "cow counties" would be under immediate squatter pressures.

Despite this relative respite from squatters for rancheros in Southern California, the expense of defending land titles before the U.S. courts drained the resources of Californios throughout the state. In 1851, Congress passed the Land Act, which required titleholders of land grants made under the Spanish and Mexican regimes to prove the validity of those titles before a San Francisco–based Land Commission. If titles were judged to be fraudulent or inadequately documented, the land would revert to the public domain and be opened to settlement under the 1841 Preemption Act or the later 1862 Homestead Act. Encouraged by the possibility that prime Californio lands could become public domain, squatters actual and fictional staked claims and made improvements in anticipation of owning the land outright. Mainly involving themselves in small-scale wheat raising, squatters and settlers alike procured passage of pro-agricultural, anti-ranching acts such as the 1872 No-Fence Law. This legislation allowed for the lawful capture of crop-eating cattle, thus forcing onto rancheros the expenses of litigation and damages or those of fencing crop fields to prevent such occurrences. Often cattle in such cases were simply shot, further reducing the value of the ranchero's herd. In addition, property tax laws exempted the state's agricultural and mining industries and heavily taxed rancho lands, including the various improvements made by squatters. As with the Land Act, these laws effected a pernicious legal distinction between Anglo farmer and Californio ranchero.[13]

Dealing with an unfamiliar legal system in an unfamiliar language proved disastrous for the land-rich but capital-poor Californios. Anglo lawyers frequently took a section of the property in payment for representing rancheros before the courts. This arrangement resulted in significant portions of the land grants leaving Californio hands as cases, often having passed on appeal through the Land Commission, federal district court, the California Supreme Court, and finally the U.S. Supreme Court, took an average of seventeen years to settle.[14] Rather than alienate land to prove title or pay taxes, rancheros would often mortgage their property to lenders who charged exorbitant rates since the property itself was uncertain collateral. If the state did not seize the property for nonpayment of taxes, financiers would foreclose once compound interest had made repayment impossible. These troubles were multiplied by the precipitous drop in cattle prices after the initial Gold Rush boom, while a series of natural disasters such as the torrential floods of 1862 and a severe drought lasting the subsequent three years depressed prices even further. Between curtailed income and skyrocketing expenses, the rancheros often lost every last acre.

By placing the burden of proof upon those who had validated land grants under Spanish and Mexican law, the very premise of the Land Act could only be to "despoil" the Californios in legal fashion, according to the novel's Don Mariano Alamar. Far from guaranteeing the equal treatment of citizens under the law, the Land Act demonstrated the use of law itself as a weapon "conquerors" would use against the "conquered":

> How could have Mexico foreseen then [in 1848] that when scarcely half a dozen years should have elapsed the trusted conquerors would, "*in Congress assembled*," pass laws which were to be retroactive upon the defenseless, helpless, conquered people, in order to despoil them? The treaty [of Guadalupe Hidalgo] said that our rights would be the same as those enjoyed by all other American citizens. But, you see, Congress takes very good care not to enact retroactive laws for Americans; laws to take away from American citizens the property which they now hold, already, with a recognized legal title. No, indeed. But they do so quickly enough with us—with us, the Spano-Americans. (67; emphasis in original)[15]

Or, as Ruiz de Burton wrote more succinctly to Mariano Guadalupe Vallejo's son Pláton, the North Americans' "boasted liberty and equality of rights seem to stop when [they] meet a Californian" (qtd. in Emparán 317).

Rather than evenhandedly adjudicating between the competing economic and political interests of U.S. citizens, the Land Act enacts power differentials according to racialized discourses of white supremacy in which Anglos are not bound to respect any rights the Californios might have in their property, despite the terms of the Treaty of Guadalupe Hidalgo.[16] What appears in U.S. nationalist discourses as the neutral adjudication of conflict among citizens is revealed as the racialized continuation of imperialism by other means, resulting in a process of colonial subject formation.[17] In José David Saldívar's words, "Ruiz de Burton writes against the grain of U.S. historiography and represents the cultures of U.S. imperialism not only as territorial and economic facts but also inevitably as a subject-constituting project" (156). As such, the U.S. legal system reflected and advanced this process of racial formation, redefining the Californios as a nonwhite population and modifying their position as citizens of a white nation. In essence, *The Squatter and the Don* no longer functions as a national allegory in that the ideal of the liberal mediation of regional, economic, and other differences are no longer operative within post-1848 U.S. nationalism for the Californios, or rather are *only* operative on the white side of the color line of which Californios increasingly found themselves on the other side.

Blushes and Political Economy

There is a sense in which *The Squatter and the Don,* even if unable to complete the project of national allegory, nonetheless secures a tentative form of whiteness for the Californios. Clarence and Mercedes eventually *do* marry, which does not prevent the loss of the rancho, the source of the Californios' independent wealth, but does halt the Alamar family's precipitous slide into a rapidly coalescing mestizo and indigenous working class.[18] Ruiz de Burton's historical romance figures the marriage between Mercedes and Clarence as the romantic union of two white people, working to mark, however provisionally, the Californios as white. These ties are made possible by the constant circulation of sentiment communicated through the blushes between the two lovers while in each other's presence. Mercedes blushes again and "again like a rose," while Clarence, not to be outdone, reddens "to the roots of his hair" continually throughout the narrative (101; 182).[19]

In *Telling Complexions: The Nineteenth-Century English Novel and the Blush,* Mary Ann O'Farrell traces the double-signification of the blush as both the visibly reliable indicator of moral character in the body's involuntary betrayal of individual will, and as a bodily practice that makes visible the social reading frame itself. In other words, the blush highlights the structures of interpretation that allow its revelation to become intelligible as such: "The use of the blush in the nineteenth-century novel . . . can be thought as articulating the tension between a sense of the blush as expressive of a deep personal truth . . . and a notion of the blush . . . as a mechanism . . . of the workings that forward the grander social work of legibility and manners" (O'Farrell 111). On one hand, the blush coordinates the invisible truth of moral character with involuntary bodily signification, aligning the legibility of character with the formation of proper individual subjectivities. On the other, the blush renders the overdetermined social relations of how character is constructed, thus revealing the legibility of the social itself. In this cultural logistics, the blush functions as a bodily discipline that ensures the individual's role in the service of maintaining and reproducing the gendered division of labor in a patriarchal social order, even when the apparently demure blush would announce the presence of an excessive, seductive desire (which, of course, typically leads to marriage).

Yet insofar as this understanding of the cultural work of the blush separates the agency of the blushing body's subjectivity and the structures of collective agency that inform the interpretation of that individual's body, something is lost in relating the cultural work of the blush in confirming collective positionalities. The blush's betrayal of an individual's sense of agency matters less than what that betrayal affirms. In some sense, the blush is not so much the denial of individual agency as much as the confirmation of the collective potentialities of agency arising out of the different racial possibilities of agency under colonialism. In this respect, O'Farrell's analysis neglects to examine the colonial context within which the blush articulates not only a politics of class but a politics of race as well. In order to foreground this terrain in *The Squatter and the Don,* I will turn to the articulation of collective economic and political agency signified by blushing effusions of the white body operative during the foundational moment of the United States.

This linking of individual subjectivity to racially nationalized positionalities finds perhaps its canonical expression in Thomas Jefferson's *Notes on the State of Virginia* (1784). Jefferson postulated that the racial differences of color "fixed in nature" between white masters and black slaves determined a self-evident distinction in each race's capacity to screen the unintended bodily effects of moral sentiment (186). Identifying the ability to blush as "the foundation of a greater or less share of beauty" in the white race, Jefferson articulated the visibility of sentiments displayed by the blush across the white face to an aesthetics of racial legibility: "Are not the fine mixtures of red and white, the expressions of every passion by greater or less suffusions of colour in the one, preferable to that eternal monotony, that immovable veil of black which covers all the emotions of the other race?" (186–87). This quote from *Notes on the State of Virginia* suggests that a profound epistemological uncertainty confronted Jefferson in reading the emotional states of African slaves. Their emotions existed, he conceded, but the "immovable veil of black" confounded the colonizers' ability to interpret the emotional states of this conscripted colonial work force (187).[20]

Jefferson's anxiously rhetorical interrogative only fitfully casts this epistemological challenge to colonial knowledge as the self-evident truth of racial ontology. In other words, by making the legibility of the blush a kind of writing, Jefferson's aesthetics of racial legibility desperately sutures the gaps in colonial knowledge. This suture provides the textual linkage between the white individual's bodily betrayal to the collective agency of whites within the new nation's political and economic registers. Only insofar as blushes constitute the legible sign of moral sentiment, blushing serves as the screen of racial legibility upon which invisible moral character is made visible upon the body. Thus the white body's ability to screen emotions across the face indicated the capacity to place private sentiments into public circulation, in contrast to the aesthetically displeasing and morally suspect stoppage of emotional economies found in the "eternal monotony" of the black slave's face. Put differently, the legibility of the blush corresponded to the racialized white subjectivity proper to the new nation's political and economic circumstances of democratic openness and laissez-faire mercantile capitalism.[21]

Insofar as the apparent inability to publish moral character via the blush indexed their position as objects within the national economy, black slaves, as the antithesis of economic and political agency, seemingly confirmed the social power of whiteness in the new nation. In contrast, the white ability to blush legibly, self-evidently, indicated, rather than any suspension of individual agency, precisely the ascension to a national collective agency. As published in blushing white faces, moral character stands as the subjectivity correlative of the structural positions of whiteness. To blush is to enact the subjective roles of agency allowed within the structural parameters of nationalized whiteness. The blushing white body is thus imagined to be the site of not only individual subjectivity but the signifier of collective national economic and political agency as well.

But precisely this nationalized conjunction of blushing white bodies and positional agency is both deployed and contested in *The Squatter and the Don*, even as the material conditions and ideological possibilities for racialized subjectivities underwent drastic changes in the transition from the early republic's mercantile capitalism to the emergent corporate monopoly capitalism of a century later. In the coalescing of post-Reconstruction nationalism around whiteness as the imperative category of civil rights and political agency, Ruiz de Burton's historical romance creates a system of circulating sentiment that enables Californio claims to whiteness by inscribing within Californio bodies the very structure of a laissez-faire, entrepreneurial, capitalist economy that might ensure continued Californio economic and political power. Blushes identify Californios as having the properly laissez-faire subjectivity for free flow of nation-building sentiment. Put differently, the circulation of blushes and blanches within the text establishes this properly white subjectivity, thereby enabling the Californios' ascension to allegorical status within the national allegory of the historical romance.

In appealing to the national aesthetics of racial legibility, *The Squatter and the Don* worked to establish whiteness for the historically mestizo, or mixed-blood, Californios, in order to regain the privileged political and economic subject-position that they had previously enjoyed. By claiming Californio whiteness through the blush, the narrative can posit the making of a truly national, bicoastal family union through marriages that no longer pose the specter of miscegenation. Simultaneously, this new national family can maintain vertical racial hierarchies in the class division of labor, with both California Indians and African Americans (represented by Mary Darrell's faithful "colored servant" Tisha) cheerfully toiling for their white patrons (59). Bereft by the 1880s of the material base of cattle ranches that had hitherto enabled a begrudged status as white within post-annexation California, the Californios found their racial identity as white ever more precarious as they collectively became wage laborers, an Indianized proletariat. Backed by the financial and cultural capital of their white in-laws, the Alamars can shift the material base of their whiteness from a failed pastoral economy hounded by legal challenges and political enemies into an entrepreneurial enterprise based upon professional employment and speculative investments in real estate, mining, banking, and the stock market.

So if by the novel's close Gabriel Alamar no longer can claim the patriarchal inheritance of the rancho as the eldest son of Don Mariano, as a banker he no longer must work as a hod carrier either. With the Alamar family married into the entrepreneurial bourgeoisie thanks to his (at long last) brother-in-law Clarence, Gabriel is able to convert a renewed class status into "whiteness," and "whiteness" into "white-collar." Even if actual Californios were not so fortunate as to be bailed out by sympathetic Anglo in-laws, the cultural work of the novel is to secure what W. E. B. Du Bois termed "the wages of whiteness" for them, and thus a relatively privileged position within post-Reconstruction U.S. nationalism. Through the historical romance's romantic unions, Californio claims to whiteness allow access to the class positions that might ensure continued Californio economic and political viability on the white side of the national color line.[22] In short, the wholesale transfer of the Alamar family from landowners to the professional classes through intermarriage highlights the process by which Californios are made white and could continue to be white within a rapidly encroaching corporate economy.

The Rise of the Soulless Empire

As the drama of contingent Californio whiteness is played out, *The Squatter and the Don* launches a critique of the national processes that ensured Californio dispossession by due process of law. This critique ultimately rests upon the narrative's insistence that the Californios had been improperly racialized as a nonwhite, conquered minority. The narrative places the Californios' dispossession by due process at the heart of the racializing allegory of proletarianization, equating the parameters of liberal consensus as the enforcement of unequal power differentials. The novel's inability to complete the necessary wedding of Mercedes Alamar and Clarence Darrell in a timely manner stands symptomatic of the contradiction between narrative insistence upon Californio whiteness and the ultimate denial of white social agency. That their wedding is abruptly canceled, severely jeopardized, and only belatedly performed highlights the ultimate dissolution of the Anglo-Californio hegemony of the immediate post-annexation period that allowed the Californios to retain some measure of political and social power even after the U.S. conquest.[23]

Despite the Californios' succession into "the wages of whiteness" through intermarriage, the very structure of white nationality remains quite tenuous in *The Squatter and the Don*. The novel ends not with the success of a reunited nation in which Californios enjoy their properly elite place but with a desperate plea for "a Redeemer who will emancipate the white slaves of California" (372).[24] Titled "Out with the Invader," the last chapter closes with a call for a mass uprising to restore the nation and release Californios and Anglo Californians alike from an imperial dependency imposed by the Central and Southern Pacific Railroads. Throughout the latter half of the narrative, this vampiric railroad monopoly emerges as an imperial force that reduces the Californios, and indeed all Californians, to "poverty, overwork and discouragement," or, in other words, to the slavery of low-paying wage labor without the prospect of upward mobility (319).[25] Ignoring its larger responsibility to the national good by arresting the invisible hand of the market, the railroad corporation figures an ominous alternative collectivity to the nation; indeed, the corporate takeover of the nation throws the very possibility of a nationalist genealogy of racialized descent into doubt. The allegory of proletarianization brought about by monopoly corporate capitalism threatens to replace a U.S. national community in which all citizens are white descendants with the debased experience of waged labor in which racial distinctions are chaotically erased in the service of imperialist postnational corporations.

This invocation of white slavery highlights the novel's claim of a juridical failure in the nature of U.S. citizenship, in that the Thirteenth Amendment's injunction against involuntary servitude scarcely stops monopoly corporations from enslaving the nation itself. Refusing to allow the struggling port town of San Diego to become the nation's second transcontinental railroad terminus upon the Pacific Ocean, the railroad monopoly ensures that "San Diego must be strangled," and along with San Diego any possibility that the Alamar family might enjoy continued economic viability as a capitalist (and not just managerial-professional) national elite (314). Don Mariano's attempts to secure such a Californio future prove disastrous as his speculative property investments in San Diego collapse in value following the Big Four's successful efforts to block the Texas Pacific Railroad.[26] In effect, enforced underdevelopment of Southern California's economy completes the dispossession of the Californios that had started with the U.S. conquest and greatly accelerated by the 1851 Land Act. Without the Texas Pacific, relates Don Mariano, "the work of ruining me begun by squatters will be finished by the millionaires" (311).

Ignoring "the wail of the prostrate South, or the impassionate appeals of California," the Southern Pacific had interfered with "the rights of the Southern people" to partake of the rapidly expanding post-Civil War capitalist economy (216; 316). Blocking the circulation of commodities onto the burgeoning Pacific Rim market, the railroad corporation hinders the trade that would realize the Californios' modernization of their economic base. For Ruiz de Burton, the machinations of autocratic corporate monopolies had replaced the democratic ideal of enlightened self-governance with the selfish, avaricious, and immoral corruption of the very governmental institutions created for the good of "We the People." The plea for liberation from white slavery in *The Squatter and the Don*, then, is not a condemnation of capitalism. After all, Clarence's entrepreneurial investments, and the Alamar family's own mercantile efforts, hold out the possibility of saving Californio whiteness. Rather, the approbation is for a government-corrupting monopoly corporate capitalism that would erase racial distinctions in the pursuit of profit. Elevating the wage labor relationship over any and all racial distinctions, the corporation monstrously endangers the white status of white people, as in the case of Gabriel Alamar.[27]

According to the narrative, the stranglehold the Southern Pacific Railroad has upon California's economy creates a crisis of embodiment in which the markings of racialized servitude have improperly been transferred from the pre-Emancipation South's black bodies to the post-Reconstruction West's white ones. What enables white slavery in California is the extent to which corporate proletarianization indiscriminately interpolated whites and nonwhites alike into a wage labor economy in a way that eroded racial distinctions.[28] In essence, the narrative protests the erasure of race in the railroad monopoly's suspension of the mercantile or entrepreneurial economy in which and from which the positions of political and economic agency accrued to nationalized white bodies. If the irony of monopoly is that a corporation devoted to the transportation of goods and people, and, indeed, symbolic of western U.S. progress itself, has become the agent of economic stagnation and stoppage, then what is perhaps even more striking is how the corporation dissolves the legible connections between moral sentiment and bodily expression.

Casting Californios and settlers alike as the victims of the monopolistic practices of the Southern Pacific, the narrative traces this immoral enslavement of whites to a peculiar lack of affect on the part of the corporation and its agents: "That soulless, heartless, shameless monster," says Mr. Mechlin, "has no soul to feel responsibility, no heart for human pity, no face for manly blush" (320). In supplanting the laissez-faire circulation of mercantile capitalism, the monopoly corporation disarticulates what had been the earlier linkage between free-market agency and the white body, destroying the legibility of race and thus national white privilege. As legally embodied yet morally unintelligible, this corporate empire transforms the economic and political agency of white U.S. citizens into the subjection of abjectly racialized human commodities. While white slavery is utterly unimaginable under the post-Reconstruction structuring of national agency around whiteness, under the narrative's characterization of the post-national corporate empire, it is the logical result of erasing racial legibility.

The railroad monopoly's apparent lack of commitment to the white nation is not limited to the attempt to erode whiteness. Draining capital from California as well as from the New South to "build railroads in Guatemala and British America," the monopolies encourage the flight of capital across national borders (370). More concerned with transnational circuits of labor and capital rather than national welfare, corporations replace the social agency of blushing white individuals with that of disembodied, deterritorialized entities that defy even their national origins. In the final chapter Ruiz de Burton quotes "a very able orator" at the California legislature's special session of 1884 that unsuccessfully attempted to force the Central Pacific to pay its taxes: "It has not occurred before in the United States that a great Commonwealth has been defied successfully by its own creatures" (369). In short, the railroad monopoly had become an *imperium in imperio*, an empire within the nation, that threatened to replace the nation's white citizenship with the corporate empire's white slavery. Delinking class difference from racial difference, corporations made white Californios into Indians, white workers into the structural equivalent of black or Chinese workers, and U.S. citizens into colonial subjects.

Facing the ongoing transnational corporate transformation of racial economies, the novel abandons the historical romance narrative altogether, as if that representational form could not negotiate the restructurings of race and class that exceed the nation's narration. In calling for redemption from white slavery, *The Squatter and the Don* suggests the historical ruin of national hegemonies imagined as white family ties secured through the legibility of the blushing body. Seemingly erasing the nation and its racialized order inscribed within blushing bodies, transnational corporations trade upon the racial and gendered division of labor at the heart of nationalism to imagine postnational groupings. Yet in some sense the supersession of the national allegory by the allegory of proletarianization may be not so much a refutation of the nation's racial formations but rather a transformation of colonialist paradigms. Transnational in its operations, the Southern Pacific Railroad becomes what Bill Brown has called "a prosthetic extension of America—not a 'natural' expression of westward expansiveness, but the mechanical institution of hemispheric domination, the technological and technocratic control over the global flow of goods" (134–35). In this sense, the experience of the Californios anticipates what would become the dominant twentieth-century mode of U.S. imperialism after the U.S.-Spanish War of 1898. The blushing individual may embody the racialized subject formation of a nationalized mercantile capitalism, but the unblushing collective of the deadly, soulless corporation enacts the logistics of colonialist and neocolonialist agency in the corporate age of U.S. empire.

Empire after California

The allegorical mappings of *eros* and *polis* in *The Squatter and the Don* register the imperial presence of monopoly corporations as they traverse national boundaries and exceed national sovereignties. If the novel mainly protests the invidious corporate racialization of whites, nonetheless, *The Squatter and the Don* also obliquely registers the subterranean resistance of racialized labor to either ranchero or corporate exploitation. This resistance comes from the Indian and mestizo ranch laborers whose presence is taken for granted and whose racialization frames Californio agency before and after 1848. The construction of these communities as objects of knowledge within national allegory's hegemonizing project has not erased all traces of persistent agency in contesting subaltern status even from within the colonial experience of exploitation. Grave as the danger posed by the transnational corporation to Californio social agency, the threat posed by racialized labor may be greater still, even if portrayed as essentially bereft of agency or community.

Indeed, Chapo, an Indian servant at the Alamar rancho, singlehandedly derails the modernist project of national allegory as completely as any monopoly corporation. Following his father's rude assault upon Don Mariano, Clarence's hasty departure from a distraught Mercedes is made possible by Chapo's studied neglect in following Victoriano's orders to groom and stable the horses "immediately": "'Yes, *patroncito*, I'll do it right away,' said the lazy Indian, who first had to stretch himself and yawn several times, then hunt up tobacco and cigarette paper, and smoke his cigarette. This done, he, having had a heavy supper, shuffled lazily to the front of the house, as Clarence was driving down the hill for the second time" (278). The resulting cancellation of the lovers' wedding jeopardizes the dream of national unity, but in a way different from Californio imaginings of corrupt antinational corporations. In this case, the immediate cause of narrative and national crisis is traced to Chapo's sense of time, as "the *Americano* went off with his horses before he [Chapo] had time to put them in the stable" (279). The narrative implies that Victoriano could have overtaken Clarence on the way to the San Diego ship docks and averted the financial disasters of the Alamar family if only Chapo had followed orders without delay. The narrative links Chapo's deficient sense of time to the racialized disposition of Indian laziness. His work habits cast the entire project of national allegory in doubt. If, for the narrative, the mark of premodernity lay in laziness, then the Indian was simply too savage to have yet internalized the bodily discipline vital to work regimes under a developing capitalism.[29]

From within the logic of the narrative, in no way could Chapo's actions be interpreted to signify an all-too-clear understanding of capitalism's restructuring of temporal (i.e., work) relations along the color line, nor laziness read as resistance to the colonizer's imposed narrative of modernity. This narrative instance demonstrates the ideological necessity of denying the foundation of Californio whiteness upon the labor of subaltern communities. Whiteness triumphant or imperiled can only be imagined as the result of the actions of true agents of history—white individuals, nations, or transnational corporations—whether legitimate or not. Hence, the narrative reveals no possibility that in coming to share the same structural and symbolic positions within the corporate U.S. imaginary, Californios and indios might also share a similar consciousness of racialized class positions. The call for redemption from white slavery, then, is what remains of the failure of post-Reconstruction national allegory. No longer able to imagine nationally relevant families, *The Squatter and the Don* is also unable to suggest alternatives to a reinscription of the nationalist wages of whiteness.

The possibility that, far from superseding the nation and its racialized order, transnational corporations trade upon the racial and gendered division of labor at the heart of nationalism to imagine other, postnational groupings fails to register for the novel. Similarly, the possibility that the very flows of labor across borders and (sometimes) color lines might provide a new basis of imagining communities, not structured according to nationality, cannot be brought to fruition. In relying upon the racialized claims of citizenship or descent, *The Squatter and the Don* demonstrates the dead end of national allegory for contesting corporate restructurings of everyday life. Rather, whether oriented North and South or East and West, the imperial nation would take the corporate form in the ensuing American Century.

CHAPTER 5

Epilogue

Decentering
National Allegory

This study has attempted to outline the nation-building discourses of late nineteenth-century U.S. national allegory as deployed and contested within the post-Reconstruction historical romance. What I have hoped to suggest is a useful mapping of the imperialist parameters of these discourses, from Henry James's nationalist epistemology of civilization and Helen Hunt Jackson's domestic scripting of Indian subjectivities to María Amparo Ruiz de Burton's refiguration of Californio racial identities. Each of these historical romances problematically stages the making of national identity as the inevitability of family ties, ties that bind North and South in a common imperial union. These allegorical remappings of *eros* and *polis* reestablish the post-Reconstruction parameters of U.S. nationalism, highlighting the role of letters in reshaping U.S. imperialist subjectivities for the turn of the century.

For the most part this study has centered upon the dominant cultures of U.S. imperialism, rather than various resistances to it, in an attempt to outline the deep persistence of such imaginings with civil society. But I would like to conclude with a brief consideration of this literature's anti-imperialist possibilities as situated within the two very different interpretive late nineteenth-century contexts of U.S. liberalism and Latin American anti-colonial thought. Although clearly moved by Jackson's historical romance *Ramona* to muse upon the plight of vanishing Indians, prominent civil rights advocate Albion Tourgée would demonstrate the limits of white liberalism in "A Study in Civilization," his 1886 review of the novel. Like Jackson, Tourgée foreclosed the possibility of indigenous incorporation into the United States and therefore shifted the possibility of indigenous inclusion within nationalism to Mexico. Casting the indigenous peoples within the United States as already extinct, "ground beneath the feet of civilized saints," Tourgée considered *Ramona* as an "angry, tender, hopeless protest against wrong" that could only "make the world mourn her loss more keenly than it would have done before" (251; 254).

Elegiac mourning of dead Indians led Tourgée to consider how the United States had dealt with indigenous peoples within its previous conquests brought up the question of the fate of those nonwhite peoples subjugated by possible U.S. imperial forays in the future, particularly (another) one into Mexico:

> In addition to the question of international right and internal policy, which such an acquisition of territory would raise, it becomes a serious consideration whether we have a right to impose our national policy of debasement and extermination upon an aboriginal population. . . . It becomes a question for every lover of humanity, whether it is better for the Indian element of the Mexican people to live in the hope of a better future under the Spanish Republic, or face hopeless degradation and inevitable extinction under the Anglo-Saxon democracy. (261)

Indian extinction was "inevitable" in the United States because U.S. democracy was racially "Anglo-Saxon" in nature: "We brought the seeds of our liberty with us from the mother country" (256). In contrast, the Mexican Republic had no "European root"; rather, "Indian hate, and the Creole sense of injustice of Spanish rule," guided by the "Mestizoes" who held out "a hand on either side to two great but decaying civilizations," wrested independence from Spain and consequently rights indigenous peoples had "never been granted under any other government" (256).[1] But insofar as Indians in the United States were concerned, rights were useless to a vanishing race. Launching an anticipatory critique of U.S. imperialism even while participating in the project of metaphoric Indian removal and thereby rhetorically consolidating past U.S. imperial conquests, Tourgée proves once again his own dictum that "Anglo-Saxon liberalism stumbles always at the color line" (257).

If Tourgée characterized *Ramona* as "not altogether a tale of *our* California" (247; emphasis in original), then Cuban expatriate José Martí would claim that Jackson had written the novel of *Nuestra América*, or Our America: "Helen Hunt Jackson, con más fuego y conocimiento, ha escrito quizás en *Ramona* nuestra novela" (203). ("Helen Hunt Jackson, with great passion and knowledge, has perhaps written our novel with *Ramona.*") Martí's subtitle of "Novela Americana" to his 1887 translation of *Ramona* into Spanish suggests the anti-imperialist possibilities he saw within the novel.[2] While Jackson's *Ramona* invidiously racialized the very population it sought to incorporate into the United States as citizens, Martí's *Ramona* presents the possibility of uniting across racial difference in a hemispheric-wide, anti-imperialist utopian community of multiracial peoples he called *Nuestra América.* This difference constitutes the gap between Tourgée's characterization of the utter impossibility of incorporating its nonwhite populations within a sense of U.S. nationhood and Martí's sense of the absolute necessity of doing so for Latin America.

Splitting the white supremacist "America that is not ours" from the "Our America" that embraced racial equality, Latin America would be saved by "its Indians" even while a genocidal "North America . . . drowns its Indians in blood" (Martí, "Our America" 85). In the balance hung not only the political independence and sovereignty of Latin American nations but, more emphatically, the very cultural and economic survival of truly American multiracial peoples in the face of "our formidable neighbor" with imperialist designs (93).[3] For Martí, the fact that Jackson was *norteamericana* did not prevent her from depicting "our people, currently scorned without reason . . . with genuine affection," a difficult task for "a famous writer among those who scorn us most" (qtd. in Retamar 703).[4] According to Martí, Jackson joined Harriet Beecher Stowe in outlining the central hemispheric social fault line of the Americas in writing to alleviate the terrible injustices faced by a racially oppressed people: "*Ramona* . . . is another *Uncle Tom's Cabin,* save without the weaknesses of Beecher's book" ("Ramona . . . es, salvas las flaquezas del libro de la Beecher, otra 'Cabaña.'"—*Traducciones* 204). In outlining racial hierarchies as the key legacy of the European colonization of the Americas, *Ramona* "gives us brothers and ideas" to imagine egalitarian societies ("El libro nos va dando hermanos e ideas"—*Traducciones* 205).

Yet if Martí credited Jackson with first envisioning this possibility, Martí's translation itself upsets the racist dynamics the English text would uphold. "Traducir es *transpensar*" ("To translate is to think beyond"), Martí once wrote (qtd. in Retamar 703; emphasis in original). Martí enacted the very antiracist project he attributed to Jackson by translating *Ramona* into Spanish. A passage from the wedding of Ramona and Alessandro illustrates Martí's translative intervention. In Jackson's original text, Father Gaspara interrogates what suspiciously appears to be the wedding of a white Spanish woman to an Indian man:

> But, as his first glance fell on Ramona, Father Gaspara's expression changed.
> "What is all this!" he thought; and as quick as he thought it, he exclaimed, in a severe tone, looking at Ramona, "Woman, are you an Indian?"
> "Yes, Father," answered Ramona, gently. "My mother was an Indian."
> "Ah! Half-breed!" thought Father Gaspara. "It is strange how sometimes one of the types will conquer, and sometimes another!" (213)

Seeking to avert certain miscegenation, Father Gaspara relinquishes only after Ramona claims Indian descent (whose maternal origin is narrated in the past tense). Yet the priest tellingly figures the mixed-blood body as the site of a continued racial struggle between colonizer and colonized that necessarily must end in the reenactment of conquest.

In contrast, Martí renders this passage thus:

> . . . el Padre Gaspar puso ojos en Ramona. "¿Qué es esto?" se dijo: y le preguntó severamente:
> —¿Eres india, mujer?
> —Sí, Padre,—respondió ella con dulzura:—soy hija de india.
> "¡Ah, es mestiza!" siguió el cura diciéndose: es raro eso de que unas veces les salga todo lo blanco, y otras todo lo indio. (*Traducciones* 399)
>
> Father Gaspar scrutinized Ramona. "What's this?" he told himself. Gravely he asked her,
> "Are you Indian, woman?"
> "Yes, Father," she replied sweetly. "I am an Indian woman's daughter."
> "Ah, she is mestiza!" the priest thought. "Seldom do mestizos appear all white or all Indian." (my translation)

Here, Padre Gaspar casts Ramona's mestiza body not as the racialized site of colonial conflict but rather as the emergence of a postcolonial rapprochement in the figure of the mestiza who morphologically favored neither parentage so exclusively. Sister to whites, Indians, and mestizos, Ramona's mestiza body confirms the fact of white ancestry but fails to privilege that ancestry over the other ancestors of *Nuestra América*. Ramona's reply in the Martí translation—which I retranslate as "I am an

Indian woman's daughter"—further indicates that the indigenous peoples of the Americas are not a matter of a lost past for Martí but rather a vital part of the hemisphere's present and future.

In this sense, what Carl Gutiérrez-Jones calls "the most blatant nostalgia" supporting *Ramona*'s "literal movement back into the colonial era and space" of Mexico City can be seen in a different light (65). Gutiérrez-Jones's comment indeed describes the ideological implications of such Indian removal from within the juridical standpoint of U.S. national borders. Taking Martí's hemispheric standpoint allows the interpretation that the novel's successful integration of criollo, mestiza, and india within the national imaginary of Mexico figures to be the first necessary step of national racial integration central to the project of making *Nuestra América*. In the American-born Felipe's marriage to Ramona despite his Spanish-born mother's objections to "such alien and mongrel blood," the penisulare's loathing of racial taint becomes the criollo's most heartfelt desire (*Ramona* 35).

In this sense, too, Gutiérrez-Jones's comment upon the following line from the novel must also be revised to take into account Martí's translation: in desiring for her daughter to grow up in Mexico, Ramona "would spare her daughter the burden she had gladly, heroically borne herself, in the bond of race" (*Ramona* 421). Gutiérrez-Jones correctly holds that Jackson's liberal reformist erasure of the mestiza Ramona as a culturally specific actor results from the juridically necessary denial of race in the U.S. context. However, in Martí's *Ramona*, this "burden of race" is lifted through Mexico's embrace of indigenous peoples in all aspects of the nation's social life, such that the leaders of late nineteenth-century Mexico would be of largely indigenous ancestry like beloved President Benito Juárez.[5] Ramona's daughter Majella not only can know her racial identity but can celebrate it as the nation's basis.[6] Translating *Ramona* into Spanish thus signified much more than crossing linguistic boundaries or even national borders. This translation also meant that nationalist paradigms of apprehension could be supplanted by anti-imperialist modes of resistance. Martí's *Ramona* imparted the visions of national union and hemispheric unity necessary to resist U.S. imperialism in the Americas. Ever aware of this seeming inevitability, Martí would caution, "The trees must form ranks to keep the giant with seven-league boots from passing" ("Our America" 85).

Martí's *Ramona* transforms the failures of U.S. liberal thought into the transnational power dynamics of racialized imperialism and subaltern resistance, and, in doing so, suggests that the structures of oppression and exploitation are not simply coterminous with the borders of the United States, although the specific institutions and local practices that mediate those relationships provide the concrete and singular forms of those experiences. Precisely this acknowledgment of the diverse manifestations of late nineteenth-century U.S. imperialism allows for the dismantling of colonial difference within interpretive practices. As Susan Gillman comments, "Martí's *Ramona* establishes the fundamentals of an adaptive reading practice, attuned to the spatio-temporal relation that is critical to comparability" (193). No longer content to repeat the terms of nationalist imperatives that enact the binary of colonizer or colonized, cultural criticism can begin to take up the question of colonial difference as the question of historical, rather than absolute, alterity. In this sense, critical practices can begin to move dialectically between critiques of U.S. nationalism and considerations of diasporic communities without sacrificing either self-criticism, resistance to racist national practices, or intervention within transnational concerns.

Put differently, critical interpretive practices can jettison literary frameworks that turn conflict into consensus, that cast the central racial struggles of the Americas into the march of hemispheric progress. Rather, the question of North and South returns, not in any nationalist sense, but instead as the unfinished project of dismantling colonial difference established by centuries of imperialism. Other ways of considering the struggles of communities (including those of the South in the North), such as Paul Gilroy's *Black Atlantic* or José Martí's *Nuestra América*, articulate human rights and cultural citizenship beyond the juridical confines of the nation, and within the forms of consciousness and transnational community conceived in the experiences of diaspora. The intensification of capital's globalization makes all the more clear the need to reconstruct cultural criticism to meet the cognitive challenges of these changes. Decentering the nation as the unexamined ground of critical analysis may displace any nationalist dreams of resistance leading to an autonomous nation. However, as long as our utopian imaginings can only take the national form, constructing affiliations either through juridical citizenship or its cultural nationalist equivalent, ethnic descent, then alternate modes of imagining communities across differences that do not heed patrolled borders will languish even as globalization advances social configurations inimical to fully human communities.

NOTES

Chapter 1

1. In the unfinished manuscript (begun in 1889) of "Tom and Huck Among the Indians," Twain does have his young protagonists go adventuring out in Indian Territory. But the Indians there are neither friendly, noble, nor vanishing; still a threat to Manifest Destiny, they remain the implacable obstacle that whites, whether Northern or Southern, must still overcome in building the nation.

2. U.S. imperialist intrigue certainly continued between the U.S.-Mexican War and the U.S.-Spanish War. In addition to the ongoing pacification of tribal nations, the most prominent examples include schemes to purchase Cuba from Spain, William Walker's Central American filibusters throughout the 1850s, the purchase of Alaska in 1867, President Grant's unsuccessful plan to annex the Dominican Republic in 1870, the 1889 Samoan Islands crisis, and the successful 1894 coup d'état in Hawaii sponsored by U.S. business interests. These events have received little analysis in terms of the way U.S. identity in the post-Reconstruction era was formed.

3. The recent critical attention to the cultures of U.S. imperialism stems from many sources, perhaps best summarized by the 1993 anthology *Cultures of United States Imperialism*, eds. Amy Kaplan and Donald E. Pease (Durham, NC: Duke University Press, 1993). Itself owing much to the postcolonial theory articulated by people of color within the United States and beyond, *Cultures of United States Imperialism* initiated a major rethinking of the role of culture in making of U.S. national identities. No longer confining U.S. imperialism to military conquest, diplomatic maneuverings, or international relations, contemporary studies of the cultures of U.S. imperialism emphasize the aesthetic, conceptual, and ideological making of imperialist subjectivities through cultural practices such as art, family life, and labor relations.

4. Among others, Nancy Armstrong's *Desire and Domestic Fiction: A Political History of the Novel* (New York: Oxford University Press, 1987) and David Miller's *The Novel and the Police* (Berkeley: University of California Press, 1988) have demonstrated how literature, particularly the novel, became a key site of bourgeois subject formation starting in the late eighteenth century. Theorists of U.S. nineteenth-century domesticity have most fully developed this line in the U.S. context; see Jane

Tompkins's *Sensational Designs: The Cultural Work of American Fiction, 1790–1860* (New York: Oxford University Press, 1985), Claudia Tate's *Domestic Allegories of Political Desire: The Black Heroine's Text at the Turn of the Century* (New York: Oxford University Press, 1992), Gillian Brown's *Domestic Individualism: Imagining Self in Nineteenth-Century America* (Berkeley: University of California Press, 1990), Karen Sánchez-Eppler's *Touching Liberty: Abolition, Feminism, and the Politics of the Body* (Berkeley: University of California Press, 1993), Laura Wexler's *Tender Violence: Domestic Visions in an Age of U.S. Imperialism* (Chapel Hill: University of North Carolina Press, 2000), and Mary Kelley, *Private Woman, Public Stage: Literary Domesticity in Nineteenth-Century America* (New York: Oxford University Press, 1984).

5. Kaplan's "Manifest Domesticity" outlines the cultural work of domestic novel in managing the racial and gender anxieties brought about by imperial expansionism; citing the works of Harriet Beecher Stowe and Sarah Josepha Hale, Kaplan suggests how the private sphere of domesticity was absolutely essential to fostering imperial subjectivities in U.S. civil society. While Romero focuses less upon the imperial role of domesticity *per se*, she does outline how white masculinist imperial subjectivities must be understood in conjunction with white male anxieties over the normalizing domestic influence of white women.

6. See Kaplan, "Romancing the Empire" and Brown, "Science Fiction, the World's Fair, and the Prosthetics of Empire."

7. The "Battles and Leaders of the Civil War" series ran in the *Century Magazine* from November 1884 through November 1887, while *The Bostonians* was serialized between February 1885 and February 1886. See Foster's account of the Civil War series, 69–70.

8. For a detailed reading of this scene, see Ann Brigham, "Touring Memorial Hall: The State of the Union in *The Bostonians*," *Arizona Quarterly* 62:3 (Autumn 2006): 5–29. James wryly noted in 1907 that the hall "dispenses (apart from its containing a noble auditorium) laurels to the dead and dinners to the living" (*American Scene* 406). It does so to this day as the dining hall for Harvard's first-year undergraduate students.

9. See Silber for a detailed contextualization of the culture of sectional reconciliation immediately after Reconstruction.

10. Michaels's discussion of *The Clansman* has greatly influenced my own reading. His extended reading of this novel can be found in his study of early-twentieth-century nativist modernism, *Our America*.

11. As Rogin has noted of the novel as well as its filmic double, the discipline of nation is directed just as much towards the New Woman as it is towards the New Negro. Rogin and Michaels have discussed how *The Clansman* and D. W. Griffith's 1915 filmic adaptation *The Birth of a Nation* formed elements (along with Supreme Court cases, historical and sociological texts, blackface minstrelsy, and other cultural practices) of a widespread realignment of the politics of race and culture within post-Reconstruction nationalism. Griffith's gesture of granting another name to his version of Dixon's *The Clansman* can be read backward, as it were, from the national future envisioned by the historical romance's Reconstruction-era Ku Klux Klan. The film's title *(The Birth of a Nation)* outlines the Progressive-Era vision of the national present as that past fulfilled. See Rogin 16–23.

12. In this sense, the list of what W. E. B. Du Bois, in *Black Reconstruction*, called the "wages of whiteness," or the innumerable, if seemingly insignificant, confirmations of white men's social, political, and economic superiority must be revised. In addition to preferential access to skilled jobs, upward mobility through professionalism, separate but clearly better public schools, parks, and hospitals, and the general sense of broad police powers over any person of color, Redemption's "wages of whiteness" included controlled sexual access to white (and black) women's bodies and the appropriation of their domestic labor in maintaining a national (white) family.

13. "Foundational fictions" is Sommer's term for the canonical historical romances of nineteenth-century Latin America. These novels articulate what Sommer has termed the "erotics of politics" underwriting the imagined communities of the nineteenth-century *criollo* nationalisms of Latin America (6). According to Sommer, foundational fictions narrate the construction of the nation as the basically inclusive consolidation of various, now-national interests within the family-making drama of the love story. Within the print medium through which the *criollo* elite could imagine the nation, unequivocal consent is figured as the natural and, above all, mutual erotic attraction between characters who represent the various "national" factions whose interests are eventually reconciled through the marriage of their representatives. Sommer's general consideration of the relationship between nation and narration has greatly informed my analysis of the post-Reconstruction historical romance.

14. Buell's controversial characterization of the United States as a postcolonial nation highlights the problems of too readily collapsing specific histories within general paradigms. In contradistinction, I would distinguish between the possibility that the liberal Creole nationalisms of the United States and other American nations may have commonalties manifested in their canonical national literatures (at least of the nineteenth century) and the assertion that the United States, as the original postcolonial nation, shares a common postcolonial situation with what Anderson terms the "Last Wave" nations of Africa and Asia. To the extent that the former is collapsed into the latter, this characterization of the postcolonial status of the United States ignores the substantial historical differences in the making of American Creole nationalisms versus those of the "Last Wave"; it also obfuscates the historical role the United States itself has played as a colonial and neocolonial power to which many of the "Last Wave" nations and even (or especially) the other Creole nations of the Americas have found themselves enthralled.

15. Fiedler casts the proclivity of characters in U.S. canonical novels to avoid the responsibilities of marriage as a form of adolescent rebellion. Huck Finn's "light out for the Territory" would be emblematic here. Fiedler diagnoses this apparent aberration of the "mature" national allegory as the "young" nation's adolescent fits of irresponsibility. This reading, however suggestive, recuperates the formal failure of national allegory as a stage in the "natural" course of national development. It also misses altogether the novel's imperialist implications.

16. Thomas Jefferson's dual role of national founding father and slave-owning father of mulatto children perhaps best exemplifies this nexus of contradictions. Correspondingly, in *Notes on the State of Virginia*, he could imagine incorporating Native Americans into the nation but not African slaves. See my chapter on *The Squatter and the Don* for my commentary on *Notes on the State of Virginia* and racialization.

17. Anderson notes how the largest American nations with correspondingly the largest slave populations—Brazil and United States—were the last to abolish slavery; Creole revolutionaries feared slave uprising even more than re-invasion by colonial powers. Brazil's literary departure from the foundational fiction paradigm is complicated by its role as the center of the Portuguese monarchy during the Napoleonic Wars. Center and periphery had in effect changed places, changing the dynamics of Creole exclusion from European centers of power. See *Imagined Communities* 47–65.

18. The distinction between civil rights and social association was central to Cable's liberalism as spelled out his essay "The Freedmen's Case in Equity." Claiming that white supremacist arguments for Jim Crow rested upon a false conflation of the two, Cable argued that the only natural ground for informal social segregation was class distinction. Ultimately, Cable's liberalism depended upon reifying class in order to avoid charges of advocating miscegenation.

19. The teleological stages of cultural evolution—savagery, barbarism, and civilization—outlined by Lewis Henry Morgan in *Ancient Society* (1877) powerfully influenced the colonial imaginary of the late-nineteenth-century United States. My chapter on Helen Hunt Jackson's 1884 novel *Ramona* gives a fuller treatment of the implications of Morgan's theories for the U.S. colonial management of Indians.

Chapter 2

1. While the imperial projects that brought about modernity began with the encounter of the indigenous peoples of the Americas and Europeans in 1492, Hobsbawm identifies this period of U.S.-European imperialism (roughly 1875–1914) as a "new kind of imperialism," a self-conscious enterprise by mostly European nations to further the expansion of industrial capital through the formal or informal control of Africa, Asia, and Latin America (56). The Berlin Conference of 1885 epitomizes this coordinated imperial division of the globe in the race for empire.

2. The canonical view of James as the expatriate individualist of complexity during a conformist age has been traced by Posnock to those liberal humanists of the 1950s (principally Trilling) who found refuge in densely situated Jamesian elaborations from vulgar determinations of literary politics (whether of the Left or the Right). Posnock's illuminating discussion of the history of James's enshrinement makes apparent the Cold War contingencies of U.S. canon formation. See 54–79.

3. According to Warren, realist literary aesthetics eventually undermined the very premises of liberal civil and social rights by showing how character and context, public and private, could not be represented and maintained as distinct without some principle of discrimination. Literary realism thus aided the establishment of whiteness as a necessary parameter of post-Reconstruction U.S. nationalism. Warren's characterization of James as aesthetically complicitous with white supremacist projects has been challenged by Michaels. For Michaels, James was essentially oblivious to the possibility that race rather than class could provide the essential basis of national social organization during the Progressive Era: "The point to be made about Jamesian realism is not that, by identifying blacks with vulgarity, it contributed to Jim Crow racism but rather that, by failing to disarticulate blacks from vulgarity, it was

unable to understand the kind of contribution Jim Crow racism was making to the reorganization of American social life." ("Jim Crow Henry James?" 289)

According to Michaels, James could not quite imagine the nation-state to be the the locus and guarantor of national "whiteness," and hence could not understand the white supremacist necessity of legislating racial difference. Making his distinctions those of class, James could not recognize, much less enact, those of race. In other words, if the state could not be imagined as the enforcer of racial distinctions, then racial distinctions did not exist; racial distinctions could not serve as a major principle of social organization short of its invidious legal recognition by the state. Michaels's analysis defines race and class as mutually exclusive organizing principles of national social life, thereby replicating Progressive radical racialism in methodologically making the same disarticulation of race and class. The complete analytical distinction between these two categories evacuates the possibility of situating James within the complex racialist remapping of post-Reconstruction U.S. nationalism and its imperial contexts, the parameters of which may be largely characterized by state-sanctioned apartheid but are not reducible to those legal distinctions.

4. In "The Significance of the Frontier in American History," Frederick Jackson Turner wrote, "Thus the advance of the frontier has meant a steady movement away from the influence of Europe, a steady growth of independence on U.S. lines. And to study this advance, the men who grew up under these conditions and the political, economic, and social results of it, is to study the really American part of our history" (4). If calls for U.S. cultural independence were at least as old as the American Revolution itself, and found its most vocal expressions in the 1830s and 1840s with Emerson's "Self-Reliance" and Noah Webster's call for a distinctly American language, then Turner's statement becomes unique for its call not for the production of U.S. culture but rather for the study of it. Turner is only the foremost of this group of self-consciously nationalist historians who emerged almost simultaneously from Johns Hopkins University and Columbia University during the 1880s and 1890s. Woodrow Wilson and William Dunning revised Reconstruction to define, during the 1890s, U.S. historiography as the emergence of the white nation. Sociologist Albion Small, another Johns Hopkins product, was extremely influential from the first organization of the field as a discipline during the 1870s and 1880s in defining American exceptionalism both as the field's methodology and its object of study. See D. Ross.

5. A key debate within U.S. feminist scholarship has been about the problematic representational relationships between nineteenth-century feminists and the racialized populations in whose name they made their political interventions. Newman's discussion is particularly helpful.

6. Ryan has also noted the departure of *The Bostonians* from the typical romance of reunion narrative, commenting, "By making a southerner the agent of this restored order, James poses an acute interpretive challenge" (270).

7. The following comment by U.S. soldier-ethnographer Richard Irving Dodge in his 1882 adventure narrative, *Our Wild Indians*, summarizes the Victorian-era assumptions about the indexing of the "spheres" to the scale of civilization: "No high order of civilization is possible without the advancement and independence of women; and in fact, the present progress of each nation and people from the utmost degradation to the highest enlightenment, can be fairly and accurately measured by the condition of its women" (345–46). Usually mustered to prove superiority of white

civilization to native savagery, the feminists of *The Bostonians* instead imply their equivalence by equating white women with black slaves. While subverting white patriarchy, this formulation leaves intact the invidious racial comparison; the complex relationship of white women to nonwhite peoples in projects of "racial reform" is treated in further detail in the next chapter.

8. Clinton's *The Other Civil War* details the general trajectory of the U.S. white feminist movement, while E. C. Du Bois's *Feminism and Suffrage* chronicles the debates within the movement over the intertwining of race and gender civil rights just before and after the Civil War.

9. If James and other cultural conservatives would view immigration as a potential threat to a sense of national feeling, then the corporations that promoted emigration from Europe to the United States during the nineteenth century had no such compulsions. Rather, employers saw immigrant labor as a way to expand production and consumption simultaneously; see Higham 14–19. Higham describes how only after the Haymarket affair in 1886 did the nativist view of immigrant labor as anti-capitalist anarchic radicals take hold within the public imagination. The violent confrontations between labor and capital in 1877, on the other hand, signified the breakdown, among the working class at least, of the free labor ideology developed before the Civil War to legitimate Northern capitalist exploitation against attacks from Southern apologists of slavery.

10. An engraving from the September 8, 1888, issue of *Frank Leslie's Illustrated Newspaper* envisioned a beleaguered Uncle Sam as the last of the Yankees on display before a jeering crowd of "foreigners," who wear the customary clothes of their countries of origin and whose business signs are in anything but English. See Burns 296 for a reproduction of Matthew Morgan's *Unrestricted Immigration and Its Results—A Possible Curiosity of the Twentieth Century: The Last Yankee*.

11. Deloria outlines the anti-modernist deployment of the figure of the Indian in elite Euro-American circles during the 1890s through the 1920s. James momentarily inhabits this trope only to dismiss it as disingenuous.

12. As Follini suggests, James's antipathy to skyscrapers also stems from a specific epistemological objection: the repetition of identical window across their façades lead to "the dominance of one particular mode of being and the oppression of one unvarying point of view" (37).

13. Griffin does further interrogate the dissolution of the Jamesian sense of national self in the face of World War I. See 149–75.

14. This Jamesian sense of women's dominance of the social field is perhaps best captured by the 1897 portrait *Mr. and Mrs. I. N. Phelps Stokes* by James's friend John Singer Sargent. Edith Stokes dominates the painting, radiant and self-assured, even as she eclipses her husband, who stands, arms crossed defensively, behind her. Sargent had originally composed the painting as a conventional society portrait, with Edith Stokes seated and attired in a blue satin evening dress. Upon seeing her, glowingly flushed by a vigorous walk, Sargent decided to depict her in a casual walking outfit, drawing, as it were, from his recognition of the energetically bodily presence in public of U.S. women. Mr. Stokes was added at the last moment to replace the Great Dane accompanying his wife in the original composition of the portrait. In a Jamesian touch, Sargent portrayed Edith Stokes with lips pursed as if to speak, while her husband remains darkly silent. See a reproduction of the painting in Banta 755.

15. As Wardley points out, Daisy Miller's choice of a somewhat questionable Italian companion indicates James's concern about possible race mixing. See her article "Reassembling Daisy Miller," *American Literary History* 3:2 (Summer 1991): 232–54.

Chapter 3

1. As Bolt demonstrates, the U.S. anti-slavery movement had its origins in opposition not only to the enslavement of Africans but to that of Indians as well. But by the 1830s, the emphasis had shifted to African enslavement in the South, given the small number of enslaved Indians and the presence of Indian slave owners. Bolt sees the post-Reconstruction Indian reform movement more as an anticipation of the Progressive movement of the turn of the century than as a continuation of radical abolition in its emphasis upon influencing government policy. See Bolt's "The Anti-Slavery Origins of Concern for the American Indians," in *Anti-Slavery, Religion and Reform*, ed. Christine Bolt and Seymour Drescher (London: Dawson & Archon, 1980). Lydia Maria Child remained interested in both abolition and Indian policy reform throughout her life, from *Hobomok* in 1824 to "An Appeal for the Indians" in 1868.

2. These critics have stressed, to differing degrees, the construction of domesticity not only within and against patriarchy but also within the national imperial endeavors of the period (1830s–1860s) known as Manifest Destiny. Romero's *Home Fronts* traces how discourses of white masculinity (such as James Fenimore Cooper's Leatherstocking Tales) constructed the national imperial impulse as a masculinist reaction to domestication by white women. Sánchez-Eppler demonstrates how the U.S. discourse of missionary work in the late nineteenth century identified U.S. children as both the object and the subjects of Christian domestication, thereby ambivalently reinscribing U.S. imperial authority in this equation of (white) children with nonwhite "savages." Wexler theorizes how the normalizing sentimental response of domestic fiction to the racial Other continuously reproduced the imperial binary which constructed that colonial difference as absolute rather than relational and historical. Taken together, these critics have challenged the notion that domesticity either formed a practice of pure resistance to patriarchy or merely replicated white male imperialist practices. Rather, the specific mediations of domesticity reveal a complex construction of social agency that empowered white middle-class women through the imperialist terms of civilization.

3. The landmark anthology *Cultures of United States Imperialism* demonstrated the implications of taking seriously the proposition that the United States has played an imperial role throughout its history. Influencing every aspect of not only how Americans practiced their beliefs of racial and cultural superiority, U.S. imperialism formed the very categories of analysis and methodological inquiry by which the U.S. academy has viewed itself and its national history. Rather than adhering to the consensus histories of American exceptionalism, which largely characterized the field of American studies during the Cold War era, *Cultures of United States Imperialism* began to address the decades-old concerns developed and expounded by scholars of color as the racialized dynamic of modernity that simultaneously granted new rights and privileges to the world's white minority and generated a colonial history of enslavement, genocide, and exploitation for the nonwhite majority. Significantly, this

methodological movement rejected the reification of imperial studies as solely the realm of political economy, military history, or international diplomacy, but examined the deep cultural work of U.S. civil society in legitimating and advancing imperialist goals.

4. In its call for reconsidering the imperial nature of U.S. domesticity, Kaplan's "Manifest Domesticity" represents a confluence of two major theoretical trends: feminist studies and postcolonial studies. Kaplan provides a theoretical corrective to the ahistorical celebration (or reductive condemnation) of women's agency through nineteenth-century domestic practices. Since her main concern is U.S. white feminism's lacuna concerning its own conditions in theorizing agency in a (post)colonial context, less emphasized is her intervention in stressing the imperial nature of all U.S. cultural practices, including those of knowledge production within the U.S. academy itself.

5. One must tread carefully between reifying the history of colonialism as a master narrative that produces identical social relations across the globe and dismissing the transnational nature of colonial relations altogether, particularly as the latter position is usually cast within the United States as American exceptionalism. Let me here acknowledge the different context of Chatterjee's enormously useful insights. Indeed the very difference between an administrative colonialism, such as that practiced by the British in India, and the settler colonialism of the United States resulted in vastly different policies. Certainly, the small number of Anglo-Indian bureaucrats, soldiers, merchants, and their families resulted in great reliance upon a British-trained cadre of mid- and low-level Indian administrators. In contrast, the vastly greater population of white settlers in the United States obviated any need to systematically educate Native Americans into the colonial administrative bureaucracy, and allowed the Indian reform movement to imagine a gradual incorporation of Native Americans into U.S. citizenship. I take this difference as an invitation, and challenge, to historicize and localize the rule of colonial difference.

6. Insofar as the national/foreign binary depends upon the public/domestic binary to generate the differential terms of the national itself, the former binary does not so much displace the latter one as much as establishes that division as the key determinant of racialized national identity.

7. Hale's support for the deportation of ex-slaves and free blacks to Liberia is perhaps most apparent in her 1852 novel *Liberia*, a key text for Kaplan's formulation of Manifest Domesticity.

8. Stowe's call for the colonization of Liberia by freed slaves in *Uncle Tom's Cabin* doubles Hale's call for deportation, even if politically they took opposite stances on abolition. What ties them is the imperial logic of domesticity, as Kaplan has shown. As Sánchez-Eppler demonstrates, the abolitionist feminist equation of slaves and white women worked through colonial regimes of representation such that white women gained a certain access to political discourses in the name of silenced slaves, thus symbolically replicating the white planter's relationship to political power in his appropriation of slave labor.

9. Griswold del Castillo chronicles the ways the U.S. Supreme Court vitiated the provisions of the Treaty of Guadalupe Hidalgo.

10. Newman documents the imperial underpinnings of nineteenth-century white feminism, showing how the question of U.S. white women's rights were formulated within a discourse of civilization and its racial hierarchies. Burton's *Burdens of*

History traces the analogous process for white British women, while Interpol Gerwal's *Home and Harem* (Durham, NC: Duke University Press, 1996) addresses not only the construction of nineteenth-century British white women's subjectivity through domestic discourses, but those of Indian women as well.

11. For example, Jackson secured an unpaid position as Special Agent to the Mission Indians in 1882, a position that allowed her to travel to Southern California. While she refused government pay on the grounds that such an action would politicize her errand of mercy, she did accept reimbursement for her travel expenses; see Mathes and Jackson's collected letters.

12. Wald analyzes how the Supreme Court decision in the Dred Scott case (1857) ensured that African Americans would exist only as property within federal law, while its decision in *Cherokee Nation v. State of Georgia* (1833) made the tribal nation vanish as an independent sovereignty within legal discourse.

13. The Jacksonian-era solution of the westward removal of tribal nations was no longer politically viable, while Congress had enacted legislation ending treaty negotiations in 1871. Nonetheless, the legislation specified that existing treaties would continue in force.

14. For reviews of this stance, see Roy Harvey Pearce, *Savagism and Civilization* (Berkeley: University of California Press, 1988); James Rawls, *Indians of California: The Changing Image* (Norman: University of Oklahoma Press, 1984); *The Destruction of the California Indians*, ed. Robert Hazier (Lincoln: University of Nebraska Press, 1993); Richard Drinnon, *Facing West: The Metaphysics of Indian-Hating and Empire-Building* (Norman: University of Oklahoma Press, 1997); and Robert Berkhofer Jr., *The White Man's Indian: Images of the American Indian from Columbus to the Present* (New York: Vintage, 1979).

15. As Wald has shown, even the designation of "dependent domestic nations" handed down by the Marshall Supreme Court in the 1831 case of *Cherokee Nation v. the State of Georgia* only anxiously asserted the superior degree of U.S. nationhood, not the invalidity of tribal nationhood.

16. The distinction between strongly intentional, blatantly race-coded segregation and an apparently harmonious blending of races was often drawn by white liberals such as George Washington Cable, who argued against Jim Crow segregation on the grounds that race or color was merely an arbitrary distinction that hindered the proper operation of class as the true grounds of social hierarchy. See his essay "The Freedman's Case in Equity."

17. For scholarly elaboration upon the development of theories of civilization during the late nineteenth century, see George W. Stocking, *Victorian Anthropology* (New York: Free Press, 1987), and his essays collected in *Race, Culture, and Evolution: Essays in the History of Anthropology* (Chicago: University of Chicago Press, 1982); Stephen J. Gould, *Ontogeny and Phylogeny* (Cambridge, MA: Harvard University Press, 1977) and *The Mismeasure of Man* (New York: Norton, 1981); Gail Bederman, *Manliness and Civilization* (Chicago: University of Chicago Press, 1995).

18. See Bhabha 85–92.

19. Chatterjee points out that precisely this differential development of the colonial state's rationalizations vis-à-vis the populations of the colonial centers and the colonies was enabled by colonial difference rather than any autochthonous, teleological expression of a uniquely Western cultural heritage lacking in the colonized areas.

20. The Ilbert bill sought to remove racial disqualifications from the 1872 version of the colonial penal code in British India, which made native civil servants ineligible to exercise jurisdiction over Europeans. A small but vocal Anglo-Indian civil society effectively negated the British Raj's rationalization of the civil service ranks in the name of preserving colonial difference, as Chatterjee notes. As Burton demonstrates in *Burdens of History*, colonial constructions of an imagined native male savagery directed against white women fueled the opposition of Anglo-Indian community (including strong organized opposition by Anglo-Indian women) to this rationalization of the colonial bureaucracy.

21. Hoxie writes that "by the end of the 1880s federal school operated on every reservation in the country. Native American education became the province of people devoted to applying modern techniques to the job of 'civilization,' and Indian schools—once an embarrassing rhetorical flourish on treaties and appropriations bills—became an integral part of the government's assimilation program" (53–54).

22. However Jackson may have seen her Indian reform work in the tradition of abolition, she clearly considered Indians as more deserving of (white) help than the freedmen. In letter written in 1880, Jackson castigated former abolitionist activist Moncure Daniel Conway for the apparent lack of abolitionist interest in the plight of Indians: "The thing I can't understand is that all you who so loved the Negro, & worked for him, should not have been ever since, just as hard at work for the Indian, who is on the whole much more cruelly oppressed; with the name of a certain sort of freedom, but prisoner in fact—left to starve, and forced into poisonous climates to die" (*Letters* 135). This racialized ranking of oppression indexes Jackson's (and, increasingly, the nation's) logic of white supremacy during the 1880s.

23. *The Hidden Power* depicts the danger of reservation-style colonial management not merely as the arbitrary rule of the Indian agent over savages (bad enough in itself); the real danger lay in the agent's despotic power over white men, and as such potential grounds for the wider abridgement of the privileges of whiteness.

24. Francis Paul Prucha's *The Great Father: The United States Government and the American Indians* (Lincoln: University of Nebraska Press, 1984) outlines the relationship between the tribes and the federal government.

25. Dundy's fellow jurist and literary critic Albion Tourgée (best known as the lead counsel for Homer Plessy in the 1896 U.S. Supreme Court case of *Plessy v. Ferguson*) would confirm in his important article "The South as a Field for Fiction" that disjuncture between one's sympathy and truly objective evaluation might exist; literary taste, unlike juridical rulings, followed "sentiment" rather than "conviction" because "romantic sympathy is scarcely at all dependent upon merit" (405).

26. I use the adjective "Darwinian" not to refer specifically to the ideas of Charles Darwin but to the new discursive universe his texts made possible. Along with Freud and Marx, Darwin is very much what Foucault termed a "founder of discursivity," or those exceedingly rare authors who "have created a possibility for something other than their discourse, yet something belonging to what they founded" (114). Certainly Darwin disavowed much of what was proclaimed in his name (particularly Social Darwinism); nonetheless the proliferation of derivative discourses in contradistinction to Darwin's particular formulations points to Darwin's foundational status.

27. Morgan's intellectual trajectory had its origins within the colonial appropria-

tion of what was imagined to be "Indian" identity and its uses for "nativizing" and nationalizing U.S. culture. See Deloria 71–94.

28. Morgan's sequel to *Ancient Society*, *Houses and House-Life of the American Aborigines*, was originally intended to be a long chapter in the former book but became a full-length monograph to allow full run to Morgan's fascination with Indian domesticity. Ultimately, Morgan's interests lay less with the present survival of Indians than with what he considered a prime opportunity to uncover the prehistory of white (specifically Aryan) civilization.

29. Delivering "The Significance of the Frontier in American History" at the Colombian Exposition in 1893, Frederick Jackson Tuner made the civilized white European's recapitulation of cultural developmental stages the process of "Americanization" itself. Adopting "savage" modes of existence best suited to the American continent, Europeans became "Indians" at first in order to become "Americans" later. If Jackson has Merrill return to the moral lessons instilled by domestic influence, Turner would make the masculine violence of the frontier necessary to nationalization. While civilized recapitulation of savagery enables the progress of civilization, savagery itself must go; the Frontier Thesis posits the genocide of Indians as the precondition for complete "Americanization."

30. A similar logic makes Huck Finn an agent of civilization in his quest to "light out for the [Indian] Territory" even if his motive is to escape Aunt Sally's attempts to "sivilize" him (321). Playing out the late nineteenth-century ethnographic equation of white children with adult Indians, *Huckleberry Finn* also hints at how the domestic project of rearing white children advances the colonial project of civilizing natives. Huck's need to "get an outfit" for this adventure of "a couple of weeks or two" ambiguously locates his performance of "sivilization" (320–21). The outfit is the product of civilization that Huck needs to rough it, the external manifestation of the concept of civilization that already forms his subjectivity. Just as the outfit is civilization (particularly its domestic aspects) in miniature, Huck's imagined distinction between himself and the Indians, who need no such outfits, constructs the colonial difference between them. If, in a certain sense, Huck plays rough-and-ready pioneer to Tom's overcivilized con man, it only signals Huck's better fitness to become a frontier settler. As Deloria has noted, playing Indian, or "roughing it," performed the cultural work of nativizing white settlers. Simultaneously, Huck's ability to travel to Indian Territory underscores his mobility as well as Indian fixity. Huck's mobility merely proves his post-cultural status and therefore worldly superiority to the Indians he will civilize through his very imperial contact with them.

31. Clearly, in the case of the suffrage movement, women sought explicitly to normalize state functioning in relation to themselves.

32. For details about the field matron program, see Emmerich's "'Civilization' and Transculturation" 33–48.

33. Alice Fletcher's career as an ethnologist of Indians associated both with the Bureau of American Ethnology and the Indian Office highlights the possibilities for unmarried white women within the governmental policy of assimilation. Fletcher was able to carve out a professional career as an expert on Indian "domestication" and even administered allotments in severalty both before and after the Dawes Act as a Special Agent for the Indian Office. She eventually received a stipend from Harvard

University as an ethnologist, becoming financially independent. Her personal life was similarly unconventional; she maintained a long-term relationship with Francis La Flesche, an Omaha Indian twenty years her junior. While her case was unique, nonetheless it reveals the extent of the possibilities opening for white women in these civilizing roles. See Joan Mark's intellectual biography of Fletcher, *A Stranger in Her Native Land: Alice Fletcher and the American Indians* (Lincoln: University of Nebraska Press, 1988).

34. Vincent Raphael has analyzed the role of white women in the "benevolent" U.S. colonial rule of the Philippines in *White Love and Other Events in Filipino History* (Durham, NC: Duke University Press, 2000).

35. The novel's disappearance of Indians from the nation and the displacement of Mexican Americans to Mexico resulted in the evermore intrusive influx of white settlers to Southern California. As Michelle Moylan has documented in her article "Reading the Indian: The Ramona Myth in American Culture," *Ramona*'s phenomenal status as a bestseller prompted heavy railroad promotion of Southern California as a literary tourist pilgrimage as well as a new homesteading destination (the Southern Pacific Railroad completed a line to Los Angeles in 1880 and to San Diego in 1884). *Prospects: An Annual of American Culture Studies* 18 (1993): 153–86. In 1891, the U.S. Congress passed an Act for the Relief of the Mission Indians, yet by then intimidation by white settlers had left only the most marginal lands available for reservations. For details on Indian land holdings in Southern California, see Florence Connolly Shipek, *Pushed into the Rocks: Southern California Indian Land Tenure 1769–1986* (Lincoln: University of Nebraska Press, 1987).

36. As a direct result of the Dawes Act, an estimated two-thirds of Indian Country was lost to white setters either through sale of "surplus" reservation lands or through sale of primary allotments between 1887 and 1934, according to Limerick 198–99. The Dawes Act also firmly established the federal government as the sole determinant of who would be considered an Indian through the generation of tribal rolls with a blood quantum threshold that determined eligibility for allotment. Although tribal nations have always recognized that community membership did not necessarily coincide with federal enrollment, several tribal nations in recent years have abandoned the federal blood quantum standard for tribal membership, including the Cherokee and the Pequot. The extent to which this move has caused widespread white resentment over the perceived privileges gained by economically successful tribal nations, without a federal criteria of racial authentication, can be measured by the attack upon the multiracial Pequot in Jeff Benedict's *Without Reservation: The Making of America's Most Powerful Indian Tribe and Foxwoods, the World's Largest Casino* (New York: HarperCollins, 2000). These anxieties are as much about the perceived lessening of white privilege to regulate the "natives" as it might be about class resentment.

37. See Bhabha 66–84.

Chapter 4

1. Recent studies pairing *Ramona* and *The Squatter and the Don* include Luis-Brown, Goldman, and Alemán. Interestingly, these studies reach quite different conclusions concerning the cultural work of these texts. Luis-Brown argues that "while

Squatter is concerned with carving out a space for Californios in whiteness, *Ramona*'s protofeminism enacts a reformist project upsetting racial norms and establishing the personhood of Indians" (62). In contrast, Goldman views *Ramona* as foreclosing a historicist critique of U.S. policy towards Indians and Californios in its adherence to the Anglo-American romance conventions of "vanishing" Others, while *The Squatter and the Don*'s heterogeneous generic nature (mixing romance, legal discourse, and political polemic) at least allows for a questioning of the generic conventions of romance that would otherwise foreclose historicist critique. Alemán writes that "both narratives consolidate whiteness" but in different ways (63). *The Squatter and the Don* situates the Californios "within a large discourse of violated rights of collective white citizenship" (72), while *Ramona* constructs "Indian identity as a biological category destined to extinction anyway" (76). My own approach focuses upon the cultural logistics these texts enable in the making and remaking of U.S. colonial difference.

2. Aranda points out the problematic erasure of Spanish/Mexican colonial enterprises in Chicana/o Studies readings of Ruiz de Burton in his article "Contradictory Impulses."

3. Castañeda has demonstrated how U.S. narratives such as Richard Henry Dana's 1840 narrative *Two Years before the Mast* constructed the Californios as half-breed barbarians. In particular, Castañeda notes how Californiana sexuality was constructed as racially repulsive and erotically enticing, simultaneously constructing myths of degenerate mestizo sexuality and the justification for the march of Manifest Destiny to the Pacific Coast.

4. For a thorough examination of these issues and others in *The Squatter and the Don*, see the essays in *María Amparo Ruiz de Burton: Critical and Pedagogical Perspectives*, ed. Amelia María de la Luz Montes and Anne Elizabeth Goldman (Lincoln: University of Nebraska Press, 2004).

5. In *Home Fronts*, Romero identifies radical alterity as the nineteenth-century construction of subjectivity as prior to, and hence outside, the operations of power. This construction of subjectivity posits an unbridgeable gap between the subject's consciousness and social change, since the former can only be protected from power by its structural isolation and the latter can only be realized through power. Romero has also noted how New Historicist readings, in following Foucault's characterization of modernity as the succession of regimes of punishment by those of discipline, replicate the modernist colonial narrative that justified genocidal campaigns against Native peoples.

6. Sommer has termed this allegorical intertwining of public interests and private affairs "foundational fictions." National allegory, in these instances, corresponds to the narration of a *criollo* hegemony, making visible the cultural negotiations by which these liberal Creole elites established a sense of national order through affective ties of mutual consensual desire between the representatives of different regional, racial, and class factions. In other words, the novelistic reconciliation of historically "internal" (once considered from the viewpoint of "the national") conflicts could be managed by the liberal Creole elites within the framework of the erotically familial.

7. That is, in a legal form unlike the property status of black slaves in the South, and so compatible with California's Free Labor status.

8. Almquist and Heizer note the similarity between the Indenture Act and one of

the notorious Black Codes enacted in Mississippi during Presidential Reconstruction. Revised in 1860 to allow for an indenture period of twenty-five years, the Indenture Act was repealed only in 1863 after this legalized slavery in a supposedly free labor state became too much of a political embarrassment during the Civil War.

9. Salvador Vallejo was Mariano Guadalupe Vallejo's younger brother. The elder Vallejo similarly participated in enslavement of Indians upon his rancho. Salvador Vallejo's Arcadian rancho mythology of happy Indian servants and wise ranchero superiors parallels the benevolent paternalism of white masters towards happy, faithful black slaves depicted in the post-Reconstruction plantation novel, indicating a certain nationalized convergence in the racialization of labor after Reconstruction.

10. Within two months of the Civil War's start, Ruiz de Burton had requested that President Lincoln promote her husband (then a captain in the Union Army) to the rank of colonel. Although at that time they had not met, Lincoln's directive to Secretary of War Simon Cameron granted her request. The text of Lincoln's letter is reprinted in Aranda's "Breaking All the Rules." Crawford documents how the Burtons circulated within elite Washington society, including befriending Mary Todd Lincoln.

11. Intermarriage served to incorporate foreigners into the Mexican Republic as citizens even as such unions helped facilitate the consolidation of Alta California's social and economic power as a virtually independent province beyond the control of central Mexican authorities during the 1830s and 1840s. To the extent that intermarriage helped consolidate Californio control over the region's economy before the Treaty of Guadalupe Hidalgo, it also gave Californios the wherewithal to maneuver in the post-1848 political landscape. The practice of Anglo-Californiana intermarriage "made the Yankee conquest smoother than it might otherwise have been" (Pitt 125).

12. Here Ruiz de Burton probably had in mind her close friend Mariano Guadalupe Vallejo's troubles with challenges to his land grant titles in modern-day Marin, Napa, and Sonoma Counties. In December 1861, the U.S. Supreme Court invalidated Vallejo's title to the huge Suscol grant under the procedures established by the Land Act. See *U.S. v. Vallejo*, 66 U.S. 541, U.S. Supreme Court, 1861. Padilla documents how Vallejo's memoir "Recuerdos históricos y personales tocante a la alta California" was annexed to Hubert H. Bancroft's collections.

13. Almaguer 45–106 documents the legislative attack upon Californio land holdings.

14. About three-quarters of the over 800 Spanish and Mexican land grants were confirmed. But by the time appeals were exhausted, legal expenses and property taxes had all but taken the land away from the original grantees. See Almaguer 66.

15. As Marlon Ross pointed out to me, Congress had indeed "taken away" property with correct legal title from U.S. citizens by the 1880s: the retroactively enacted Thirteenth Amendment (ratified in 1865), which outlawed chattel slavery.

16. Ruiz de Burton was most likely aware of the 1859 petition to Congress signed by over fifty Californios. Outlining many of the same circumstances that had already economically devastated the rancheros, the petitioners pleaded for Congress to "respect, protect, and uphold the treaty of Guadalupe Hidalgo" (Cleland 243). The utter lack of response to this plea is reflected in Don Mariano's resignation to fall victim to the "sins of our legislators" (*The Squatter and the Don* 329).

17. What I term "dispossession by due process" resonates with Carl Gutiérrez-Jones's characterization of the liberal distinction between force and consent. As

Gutiérrez-Jones notes, Chicana/o narrative recasts liberalism's consent/force dichotomy into the hegemony/coercion parameters of power (44). With consent supposedly represented by legislation so clearly aligned with the violence of conquerors, *The Squatter and the Don* accurately diagnoses the racialized parameters of U.S. legal practices. Yet, as I have suggested here and elsewhere, the novel's critique fails to transform this realization into viable strategies of communal resistance along lines other than an imagined, shared whiteness.

18. The novel's solution to the proletarianization of the Alamar family is an aesthetic resolution of an unresolvable historical dynamic, as Sánchez and Pita have pointed out. Yet the specific way this aesthetic resolution is enacted and legitimated outlines the historical limitations (as well as possibilities) of imagining resistant practices.

19. There are literally dozens of examples of blushing and blanching scattered throughout the narrative, but the dispersed nature of their narration will limit my direct quotation to these passages.

20. The same epistemological uncertainty confronted British inquiries into the usefulness of blushing in revealing the emotional status of colonial subjects. In his 1872 treatise upon the physiological manifestations of emotions upon the human body, Darwin reported that the observations of a British colonial official in India were frustrated by those under his surveillance. The colonial official "attended to the expression of the inhabitants, but found much difficulty in arriving at any safe conclusions, owing to their habitual concealment of all emotions in the presence of Europeans" (21).

21. Laissez-faire at least compared to the restrictive trade measures the British metropole—like other imperial centers—had placed upon its colonial periphery.

22. As Roediger and Lipsitz have shown for the nineteenth- and twentieth-century United States respectively, a white proletariat gained material and symbolic advantages over a nonwhite proletariat. Roediger examines the nineteenth-century construction of whiteness, while Lipsitz theorizes the continued hegemonic understanding of its value in *The Possessive Investment in Whiteness: How White People Profit from Identity Politics* (Philadelphia: Temple University Press, 1998).

23. According to Sánchez and Pita, the cancellation of the wedding because of the conflict between squatter William Darrell and Don Mariano Alamar is a narrative ruse that cannot hide even greater structural contradictions. My own reading considers the cancellation of the wedding as symptomatic of a somewhat different condition as noted later.

24. The use of the term "Redeemer" in this context marks the ambivalent positioning of the cultural work Ruiz de Burton's narrative performs. On one hand, Redeemer invokes topological imaginings of Christian salvation, and, more specifically in the immediate post–Civil War era, Lincoln's Emancipation Proclamation; on the other, the Redeemers also refers to the group of Whiggish Southern Democrats whom early historians of the New South enshrined as the liberators of a distraught white South from the ravages of "black misrule." The uneasy ambivalence of the term in the post-Reconstruction period suggests the treacherous parameters of race and class that *The Squatter and the Don* attempts to negotiate in creating a place for the Californios within the post-Reconstruction white nation.

25. Ruiz de Burton's critique of the railroad monopolies stands as an early exam-

ple of muckraking, one example of the populist reaction to the emerging dominance of monopoly capitalism in U.S. cultural and political life. While other examples of literary muckraking are much better known—such as Upton Sinclair's 1905 novel *The Jungle*, a fictionalized exposé of the Chicago meat packing industry—*The Squatter and the Don* suggests that the disparate impact of monopolistic practices upon a Californio elite precipitated Ruiz de Burton's muckraking response somewhat before the practice became a widespread response to monopoly capitalism.

26. As Sánchez and Pita note, Ruiz de Burton herself lost out in a similar speculative bid.

27. The narrative's trajectory from decrying Gabriel's racializing wage labor to protesting the monopoly's white slavery stands in marked contrast to Roediger's description of the white working class's movement from the rhetoric of white slavery in the 1840s to the one of wage slavery after the Civil War. Before Emancipation, white slavery denoted not a challenge to capitalist labor relations but an expression of *Herrenvolk* Republican objections to the capitalist (mis)treatment of white workers as if they were black slaves. The use of the phrase "white slavery" helped consolidate a racialized labor ideology of white identity in forging a "free labor" working class. In Roediger's words, "use of a term like white slavery was not an act of solidarity with the slave but rather a call to arms to end the inappropriate oppression of whites" (68). "Wage slavery," on the other hand, implied bondage as the inherent condition of a capitalist system of wage labor. Only after the Civil War did elements of the white working class take up widespread usage of the term as the Republican "free labor" formulation lost its tenability in the face of the large-scale emergence of permanent wage laborers. The term "white slavery" disappeared from the vocabulary of the white working class, and by the turn of the century had come to denote the supposedly widespread and lurid international conspiracy to force white women to become prostitutes for nonwhite men in foreign lands.

28. Michaels has convincingly argued that the post-Reconstruction national imagination subsumed class antagonisms as well as other differences of region and politics under the sign of racial solidarity (i.e., white supremacy) in the making of Progressive-Era U.S. nationalism. See his study of nativist modernism, *Our America*. Under such a formulation, "white slavery" of the by-definition white citizenry is not even a possibility, while the "slavery" of nonwhites could not only be carried out de facto but indeed celebrated in plantation novels and the California Mission revival.

29. See Hurtado's *Indian Survival on the California Frontier* for a more detailed account of how California Indians negotiated wage labor relations to their own ends after the U.S. conquest.

Chapter 5

1. Tourgée's analysis of Mexican nationalism anticipates Anderson's in its focus upon *criollo* resentment and their fear of Indian uprisings.

2. See Lomas for fascinating interpretation of Martí's translation of *Ramona* as the prefiguration of "a Latino/a insurgency of natives and migrants," not least of all in the "theorizing of possible alliances among diverse communities and against an institutionalized Anglo-supremacism" (262).

3. Exiled in 1870 from Cuba for supporting the 1868 uprising against Spanish colonial rule, Martí would live in New York City between 1881 and 1895, all the while continuing to work towards Cuban independence. He died fighting for that cause in 1895 during the Second War of Independence.

4. The original: "nuestra raza, a menudo desdeñada sin razón, tratada con tan ingeno afecto, y en toda su bondad reconocida, por una escritora famosa entre los que más nos desdeñan." Unless otherwise noted, all translations are mine.

5. That reviled dictator Porfirio Díaz was also of indigenous background does not obviate Martí's project; racial integration of the nation might be the first step towards *Nuestra América* but not the last. During the Porfiriato (1876–1911), Mexico became ensconced in extensive neocolonial relations with U.S. capital, precisely the situation (besides outright imperial control) that Martí fought against and that Tourgée warned would provide a rationale for barefaced U.S. imperialism.

6. Gillman traces the full implications of Martí's articulation of the reform traditions of Jackson and Stowe.

WORKS CITED

Alemán, Jesse. "Historical Amnesia and the Vanishing Mestiza: The Problem of Race in *The Squatter and the Don* and *Ramona*." *Aztlán* 27:1 (Spring 2002): 59–93.

Almaguer, Tomás. *Racial Fault Lines: The Historical Origins of White Supremacy in California*. Berkeley: University of California Press, 1994.

Almquist, Alan F., and Robert F. Heizer. *The Other Californians: Prejudice and Discrimination under Spain, Mexico, and the United States to 1920*. Berkeley: University of California Press, 1971.

Anderson, Benedict. "Holy Perversions: Nationalism in Last Wave and Creole Novels." Nationalism and Sexualities Conference, Harvard University, June 17, 1989.

———. *Imagined Communities: Reflections on the Origin and Spread of Nationalism*. New York: Verso, 1991.

Aranda, José, Jr. "Breaking All the Rules: María Amparo Ruiz de Burton Writes a Civil War Novel." In *Recovering the U.S. Hispanic Literary Heritage, Vol. III*, edited by María Herrera-Sobek and Virginia Sánchez-Korrol, 61–73. Houston: Arte Público Press, 2000.

———. "Contradictory Impulses: María Amparo Ruiz de Burton, Resistance Theory, and the Politics of Chicana/o Studies." *American Literature* 70:3 (September 1998): 551–80.

Banta, Martha. *Imaging American Women: Ideas and Ideals in Cultural History*. New York: Columbia University Press, 1987.

Benjamin, Walter. *The Origin of German Tragic Drama*. New York: Verso, 1977.

Bhabha, Homi K. *The Location of Culture*. New York: Routledge, 1994.

Blair, Sara. *Henry James and the Writing of Race and Nation*. Cambridge: Cambridge University Press, 1996.

Brown, Bill. "Science Fiction, the World's Fair, and the Prosthetics of Empire." In *Cultures of U.S. Imperialism*, edited by Donald Pease and Amy Kaplan, 129–63. Durham, NC: Duke University Press, 1993.

Buell, Lawerence. "American Literary Emergence as a Postcolonial Phenomenon." *American Literary History* 4:3 (Fall 1992): 411–42.

Burns, Sarah. *Pastoral Inventions: Rural Life in Nineteenth-Century American Art and Culture*. Philadelphia: Temple University Press, 1989.

Burton, Antoinette. *Burdens of History: British Feminists, Indian Women, and Imperial Culture, 1865–1925.* Chapel Hill: University of North Carolina Press, 1994.

Cable, George Washington. "The Freedman's Case in Equity." In *The Negro Question*, 49–74. New York: Doubleday Anchor, 1958.

———. *The Grandissimes.* New York: Penguin, 1988.

Castañeda, Antonia. "The Political Economy of Nineteenth Century Stereotypes of Californianas." In *Between Borders: Essays on Mexicana/Chicana History*, edited by Adelaida R. Del Castillo, 213–36. Encino, CA: Floricanto Press, 1990.

Chatterjee, Partha. *The Nation and Its Fragments: Colonial and Postcolonial Histories.* Princeton, NJ: Princeton University Press, 1993.

Child, Lydia Maria. "An Appeal for the Indians." In *A Lydia Maria Child Reader*, edited by Carolyn Karcher, 79–94. Durham, NC: Duke University Press, 1997.

Cleland, Robert Glass. *The Cattle on a Thousand Hills: Southern California 1850–1880.* San Marino, CA: Huntington Library, 1951.

Clinton, Catherine. *The Other Civil War: American Women in the Nineteenth Century.* New York: Hill & Wang, 1986.

Crawford, Kathleen. "María Amparo Ruiz de Burton: The General's Lady." *Journal of San Diego History.* 30:3 (1984): 198–211.

Darwin, Charles. *The Expression of the Emotions in Man and Animals.* Chicago: University of Chicago Press, 1965.

Deloria, Philip. *Playing Indian.* New Haven, CT: Yale University Press, 1998.

Dixon, Thomas. *The Clansman: A Historical Romance of the Ku Klux Klan.* Lexington: University Press of Kentucky, 1970.

Dodge, Richard Irving. *Our Wild Indians.* Hartford, CT: A. D. Worthington, 1890.

Du Bois, Ellen Carol. *Feminism and Suffrage: The Emergence of an Independent Women's Movement in America 1848–1869.* Ithaca, NY: Cornell University Press, 1978.

Du Bois, W. E. B. *Black Reconstruction in America 1860–1880.* New York: Atheneum, 1992.

Eliot, T. S. "Henry James: In Memory." In *The Shock of Recognition: The Development of Literature in the United States, Recorded by the Men Who Made It,* vol 2. edited by Edmund Wilson, 2:853–65. New York: Farrar Straus and Cudahay, 1955.

Elk v. Wilkins, 112 US 94. Supreme Court of the United States. 1884 U.S. Supreme Court Cases & Opinions. U.S. Supreme Court Center web. 27 July 2008.

Emmerich, Lisa E. "'Civilization' and Transculturation: The Field Matron Program and Cross-Cultural Contact." *American Indian Culture and Research Journal* 15:4 (1991): 33–48.

Emparán, Madie Brown. *The Vallejos of California.* San Francisco: University of San Francisco Greeson Library Associates, 1968.

Fiedler, Leslie. "Come Back to the Raft Ag'in, Huck Honey!" In *Adventures of Huckleberry Finn*, edited by Gerald Graff and James Phelan, 528–34. Boston: Bedford, 1995.

Fischer, Victor. "Huck Finn Reviewed: The Reception of *Huckleberry Finn* in the United States, 1885–1897." *American Literary Realism* 16:1 (1983): 1–57.

Follini, Tamara L. "Habituations of Modernism: Henry James's New York, 1907." *Cambridge Quarterly* 37:1 (2008): 30–46.

Foster, Gaines. *Ghosts of the Confederacy: Defeat, the Lost Cause, and the Emergence of the New South, 1865–1913*. New York: Oxford University Press, 1987.

Foucault, Michel. "What Is an Author?" In *The Michel Foucault Reader*, edited by Paul Rabinow, 101–20. New York: Pantheon, 1984.

Freedman, Jonathan. "Introduction: The Moment of Henry James." In *The Cambridge Companion to Henry James*, 1–20. New York: Cambridge University Press, 1998.

Gates, Merrill E. "Land and Law as Agents in Educating Indians." In *Americanizing the American Indians: Writings by "Friends of the Indian," 1880–1900*, edited by Francis Paul Prucha, 45–56. Cambridge, MA: Harvard University Press, 1973.

Gillman, Susan. "Otra vez Caliban/Encore Caliban: Adaptation, Translation, Americas Studies." *American Literary History* 20:1–2 (Spring/Summer 2008): 187–209.

Gilroy, Paul. *The Black Atlantic: Modernity and Double Consciousness*. Cambridge, MA: Harvard University Press, 1993.

Goldman, Anne E. "'I think our romance is spoiled,' or, Crossing Genres: California History in Helen Hunt Jackson's *Ramona* and María Amparo Ruiz de Burton's *The Squatter and the Don*." In *Over the Edge: Remapping the American West*, edited by Valerie Matsumoto and Blake Allmendinger, 65–84. Berkeley: University of California Press, 1999.

Graham, Wendy. "Notes on a Native Son: Henry James's New York." *American Literary History* 21:2 (Summer 2009): 239–67.

Griffin, Susan M. *The Historical Eye: The Texture of the Visual in Late James*. Boston: Northeastern University Press, 1991.

Griswold del Castillo, Richard. *The Treaty of Guadalupe Hidalgo: A Legacy of Conflict*. Norman: University of Oklahoma Press, 1990.

Gutiérrez-Jones, Carl. *Rethinking the Borderlands: Between Chicano Culture and Legal Discourse*. Berkeley: University of California Press, 1995.

Guy, Donna J. "'White Slavery,' Citizenship and Nationality in Argentina." In *Nationalities and Sexualities*, edited by Andrew Parker, Mary Russo, Doris Sommer, and Patricia Yeager, 201–17. New York: Routledge, 1992.

Harris, Joel Chandler. "*Huckleberry Finn* and His Critics." *Atlanta Constitution*, May 26, 1885, p. 4.

Higham, John. *Strangers in the Land: Patterns of American Nativism, 1860–1925*. New York: Atheneum, 1978.

Hobsbawm, Eric. *The Age of Empire, 1875–1914*. New York: Vintage, 1989.

Hoxie, Frederick. *A Final Promise: The Campaign to Assimilate the Indians, 1880–1920*. Lincoln: University of Nebraska Press, 1984.

Hurtado, Albert L. *Indian Survival on the California Frontier*. New Haven, CT: Yale University Press, 1988.

Jackson, Helen Hunt. *A Century of Dishonor*. Norman: University of Oklahoma Press, 1995.

———. *Glimpses of Three Coasts*. Boston: Roberts Brothers, 1886.

———. *The Indian Reform Letters of Helen Hunt Jackson 1879–1885*. Edited by Valerie Sherer Mathes. Norman: University of Oklahoma Press, 1998.

———. *Ramona*. Boston: Little, Brown, 1939.

James, Henry. "The American Novel of Dialect." In *Literary Criticism: Essays on Literature, American Writers, English Writers*, 696–702. New York: Library of America, 1984.

———. *The American Scene.* In *Collected Travel Writings: Great Britain and America*, 353–736. New York: Library of America, 1993.
———. *The Bostonians.* New York: Library of America, 1991.
———. *The Complete Notebooks of Henry James.* New York: Oxford University Press, 1987.
———. *Letters.* Edited by Leon Edel. 4 vols. Cambridge, MA: Harvard University Press, 1974–84.
———. "The Manners of American Women." In *The Restless Analyst*, edited by Peter Buitenhuis, 207–56. Toronto: Roger Ascham, 1979.
———. "A New England Winter." In *Complete Stories 1884–1891*, 65–122. New York: Library of America, 1999.
———. "The Point of View." In *Complete Stories 1874–1884*, 519–64. New York: Library of America, 1999.
———. Preface. *The Portrait of a Lady.* By Henry James. In *Literary Criticism: French, Other European Writers, Prefaces to the New York Edition.* New York: Library of America, 1984. 1070–85.
———. *A Small Boy and Others.* Princeton, NJ: Princeton University Press, 1983.
———. *The Question of Our Speech and the Lesson of Balzac.* Boston: Riverside, 1905.
———. "The Speech of American Women." In *The Restless Analyst*, edited by Peter Buitenhuis, 165–204. Toronto: Roger Ascham, 1979.
———. "The Story of a Year." In *Complete Stories 1864–1874.* New York: Library of America, 1999. 23–66.
Jefferson, Thomas. *Notes on the States of Virginia.* In *The Portable Thomas Jefferson*, edited by Merrill Peterson, 23–232. New York: Penguin, 1988.
Kaplan, Amy. "Manifest Domesticity." *American Literature* 70:3 (September 1998): 581–606.
Kaplan, Amy, and Donald E. Pease, eds. *Cultures of United States Imperialism.* Durham, NC: Duke University Press, 1993.
Kreyling, Michael. "Introduction." *The Grandissimes* by George Washington Cable, vii–xx. New York: Penguin, 1988.
Limerick, Patricia. *The Legacy of Conquest: The Unbroken Past of the American West.* New York: W. W. Norton, 1987.
Lomas, Laura. *Translating Empire: José Martí, Migrant Latino Subjects, and American Modernities.* Durham, NC: Duke University Press, 2008.
Luis-Brown, David. *Waves of Decolonization: Discourses of Race and Hemispheric Citizenship in Cuba, Mexico, and the United States.* Durham, NC: Duke University Press, 2008.
Martí, José. "'Ramona,' de Helen Hunt Jackson." In *Obras Completas: Traducciones.* Vol. 24, 199–205.. La Habana: Editorial Nacional de Cuba, 1965.
———. "Our America." In *Our America: Writings on Latin America and the Struggle for Cuban Independence*, edited by Philip S. Foner, 84–94. New York: Monthly Review Press, 1977.
Mathes, Valerie Sherer. *Helen Hunt Jackson and Her Indian Reform Legacy.* Austin: University of Texas Press, 1990.
Matthiessen, F. O. *The James Family.* New York: Knopf, 1961.
Melville, Herman. *The Confidence Man.* New York: Oxford University Press, 1999.

Michaels, Walter Benn. "Jim Crow Henry James?" *Henry James Review* 16 (1995): 273–77.

———. *Our America: Nativism, Modernism, Pluralism.* Durham, NC: Duke University Press, 1995.

———. "The Souls of White Folk." In *Literature and the Body: Essays on Populations and Persons*, edited by Elaine Scarry, 185–209. Baltimore: Johns Hopkins University Press, 1988.

Morgan, Lewis Henry. *Ancient Society.* Tucson: University of Arizona Press, 1985.

Morrison, Toni. *Playing in the Dark: Whiteness and the Literary Imagination.* New York: Vintage, 1993.

Newman, Louise. *White Women's Rights: The Racial Origins of Feminism in the United States.* New York: Oxford University Press, 1999.

North, Michael. *The Dialect of Modernism: Race, Language and Twentieth-Century Literature.* New York: Oxford University Press, 1994.

O'Farrell, Mary Ann. *Telling Complexions: The Nineteenth-Century English Novel and the Blush.* Durham, NC: Duke University Press, 1997.

Padilla, Genaro. *My History, Not Yours: The Formation of Mexican American Autobiography.* Madison: University of Wisconsin Press, 1993.

Pancoast, Henry S. *The Indian before the Law.* Philadelphia: Indian Rights Association, 1884.

Pitt, Leonard. *The Decline of the Californios: A Social History of the Spanish-Speaking Californians, 1846–1890.* Berkeley: University of California Press, 1966.

Posnock, Ross. *The Trial of Curiosity: Henry James, William James, and the Challenge of Modernity.* New York: Oxford University Press, 1991.

Renan, Ernest. "What Is a Nation?" In *Nation and Narration*, edited by Homi K. Bhabha, 8–22. New York: Routledge, 1990.

Retamar, Roberto Fernandez. "Sobre *Ramona* de Helen Hunt Jackson y José Martí." In *Mélanges a la Mémoire D'André Jouch-Ruan.* Vol. 2, 699–705. Provence: Editions de l'Université de Provence, 1978.

Roediger, David R. *The Wages of Whiteness: Race and the Making of the American Working Class.* New York: Verso, 1991.

Rogin, Michael. "'The Sword Became a Flashing Vision': D. W. Griffith's *The Birth of a Nation.*" In *The New American Studies: Essays from Representations*, edited by Philip Fisher, 346–91. Berkeley: University of California Press, 1991.

Romero, Lora. *Home Fronts: Domesticity and Its Critics in the Antebellum United States.* Durham, NC: Duke University Press, 1997.

Ross, Dorothy. *The Origins of American Social Science.* New York: Cambridge University Press, 1997.

Ross, Marlon. Personal communication, 10 October 1998.

Ruiz de Burton, María Amparo. *The Squatter and the Don.* Houston: Arte Público Press, 1992.

———. *Who Would Have Thought It?* Houston: Arte Público Press, 1995.

Ryan, Susan M. "*The Bostonians* and the Civil War." *The Henry James Revew* 26 (2005): 265–72.

Saldívar, José David. *Border Matters: Remapping American Cultural Studies.* Berkeley: University of California Press, 1997.

Sánchez, Rosaura. *Telling Identities: The Californio Testimonios.* Minneapolis: University of Minnesota Press, 1995.
Sanchez, Rosaura, and Beatrice Pita. "Introduction." *The Squatter and the Don.* Ny María Amparo Ruiz de Burton, 5–51. Houston: Arte Público Press, 1992.
Sánchez-Eppler, Karen. "Raising Empires Like Children: Race, Nation and Religious Education." *American Literary History* 8:3 (Fall 1996): 399–425.
Schurz, Carl. "Present Aspects of the Indian Problem." *North American Review* 133.296 (July 1881): 1–24.
Silber, Nina. *The Romance of Reunion: Northerners and the South, 1865–1900.* Chapel Hill: University of North Carolina Press, 1993.
Sommer, Doris. *Foundational Fictions: The National Romances of Latin America.* Berkeley: University of California Press, 1991.
Tibbles, Thomas Henry. *The Hidden Power.* New York: Carelton & Co., 1881.
———. *Standing Bear and the Ponca Chiefs.* Edited by Kay Graber. Lincoln: University of Nebraska Press, 1995.
Tourgée, Albion W. *Bricks Without Straw.* Ridgewood, NJ: Gregg Press, 1967.
———. "The South as a Field for Fiction." *Forum* 6 (December 1888): 404–13.
———. "A Study in Civilization." *North American Review* 143:3 (September 1886): 246–61.
Turner, Frederick Jackson. "The Significance of the Frontier in American History." In *The Frontier in American History.* Tucson: University of Arizona Press, 1992.
Twain, Mark. *The Adventures of Huckleberry Finn.* New York: Penguin, 1987.
———. *A Connecticut Yankee at King Arthur's Court.* New York: Penguin, 1986.
———. "Huck Finn and Tom Sawyer Among the Indians." In *Huck Finn and Tom Sawyer Among the Indians and Other Unfinished Stories*, 33–81. Berkeley: University of California Press, 1989.
Vallejo, Guadalupe. "Ranch and Mission Days in Alta California." *Century Magazine* (December 1890): 183–92.
Wald, Priscilla. *Constituting Americans: Cultural Anxiety and Narrative Form.* Durham, NC: Duke University Press, 1995.
Wardley, Lynn. "Woman's Voice, Democracy's Body, and *The Bostonians.*" *ELH* 56:3 (1989): 639–65.
Warren, Kenneth. *Black and White Strangers: Race and American Literary Realism.* Chicago: University of Chicago Press, 1993.
Wexler, Laura. *Tender Violence: Domestic Visions in an Age of U.S. Imperialism.* Charlotte, NC: University of North Carolina Press, 2000.
Wilson, Benjamin Davis. *The Indians of Southern California in 1852.* University of Nebraska Press, 1995.

INDEX

abolitionism: compared with Indian reform movement, 51, 65–66, 122n22; and enslaved Indians, 119n1; and gender oppression, 31; and North-South relations, 32; and Phillips, 51, 69; white women's involvement in, 27, 30, 31, 32, 52, 120n8. *See also* slavery
"Accent of the Future" (James), 29, 41
Across the Chasm (Magruder), 6
The Adventures of Huckleberry Finn (Twain), 1–3, 10, 12, 23–24, 115n15, 123n30
African Americans. *See* blacks
Alaska, 113n2
Alemán, Jesse, 124–25n1
Almaguer, Tomás, 126n13
Almquist, Alan F., 125–26n8
amendments. *See specific Constitutional amendments*
"American Letters" (James), 21–22
"The American Novel of Dialect" (James), 21–22, 24–26, 28
The American Scene (James): "Accent of the Future" in, 29, 42; on Du Bois, 28; on English language, 44–45; on Harvard University's Memorial Hall, 114n8; on immigrants, 35–38, 40, 41–45; on Irving's house, 40; on modernity, 36–42; publication of, 3; on ruins, 1; on skyscrapers, 39–40, 42–43; on South and Southern, 28; on women's preeminence, 19, 46–47
Ancient Society (Morgan), 72–74, 78, 116n19, 123n28
Anderson, Benedict, 10, 11, 34, 115n14, 116n17, 128n1
anthropology, 56, 59, 72–74, 83
anti-slavery movement. *See* abolitionism
Apache, 67. *See also* Indians
"An Appeal for the Indians" (Child), 79
Aranda, José, Jr., 92, 125n2, 126n10
Armstrong, Nancy, 113n4
assimilation, 57–60, 83–84, 123–24n33
Atalanta in the South (Elliott), 6
Athenaeum, Boston, 39
Atlanta Constitution, 24
Atlantic Monthly, 23, 30, 65

Benedict, Jeff, 124n36
Bhabha, Homi, 59–60, 84
The Birth of a Nation, 114n11
Black Atlantic (Gilroy), 112
Black Codes, 126n8
blacks: and Black Codes, 128n8; in Cable's *The Grandissimes*, 14–15; deportation of, to Liberia, 54, 121nn7–8; legal status of, 65–66, 71–72; lynching of black men, 5, 8, 17, 28; and miscegenation, 15, 35, 116n18; quadroon mistress in

Cable's *The Grandissimes*, 13, 14; racial equality and civil rights for, 15, 23, 66, 116n18; rape by black men, 58; rape of black women, 5, 8, 11, 17; in Ruiz de Burton's *The Squatter and the Don*, 99; suffrage for, 32–32. *See also* Jim Crow segregation; slavery

Blair, Sara, 23, 29

The Bloody Chasm (DeForest), 6

blushing, 96–100, 103, 104, 127nn19–20

Bolt, Christine, 119n1

The Bostonians (James): as American tale, 29–31; ending of, 33–34; failure of, 30; feminist movement in, 19, 27, 31–35, 46–47, 118n7; gender relations in, 31, 33–35; Harvard University's Memorial Hall in, 6, 114n8; on immigrants, 43; James's interest in revision of, 30; James's refusal to write in dialect in, 18, 29, 34–35; marriage in, 19, 33–34; Elizabeth Peabody's fictional rendition in, 30; plans for writing of, 47; publishers of, 29–30; Ransom as representation of white masculinity in, 34; representational failures in, 18–19, 34–35; as romance of reunion, 3–4, 6, 11, 18–19, 31, 33–34, 107, 117n6; romantic pairing of Northerner and Southerner in, 6, 31, 33–34, 117n6; serialization of, in *Century Magazine*, 5, 23, 29–30, 115n7; Stowe's fictional rendition in, 26

Bourget, Paul, 25

Brazil, 116n17

Bricks Without Straw (Tourgée), 61

Brown, Bill, 3, 104

Brueton's Bayou (Habberton), 6

Bryn Mawr College, 45–46

Buell, Lawrence, 115n14

Burton, Antoinette, 120–21n10, 122n20

Burton, Henry S., 92

Cable, George Washington, 5, 12–16, 23, 116n18, 121n16

California: Burton family property in, 92; colonial difference in, 85–88; Gold Rush in, 90, 94, 95; Indian labor force in, 77–78, 82, 89–91, 125–26nn7–9, 128n29; Jackson's investigation of Mission Indians in, 74–76; missionaries and missions in, 19, 75–76, 89, 119n2; natural disasters in, 95; railroad in, 20, 91, 93, 101–6; ranchos and rancheros in, 89–90, 93–96, 104–6, 126n9; as setting of Jackson's *Ramona*, 62, 85–86; Spanish and Mexican land grants in, 86, 94–95, 126nn12–14; U.S. conquest of, 90. *See also* Californios; Mission Indians; *Ramona* (Jackson); *The Squatter and the Don* (Ruiz de Burton)

Californios: decline of, 89–91, 93–96, 99, 101, 103; land loss of, 93–96, 100, 101, 126n12, 126n14; marriage between Anglos and, 19–20, 89, 92–93, 96, 99–101, 104–5, 126n11; as mestizos, 90; petition to U.S. Congress by, 126n16; whiteness of, 19–20, 87, 89–91, 96, 99–101, 105–6, 124–25n1

Cameron, Simon, 126n10

capitalism. *See* railroad

Castañeda, Antonia, 125n3

Century Magazine, 5, 15, 23, 29–30, 114n7

A Century of Dishonor (Jackson), 62–63, 74, 75, 76

Cervantes, Miguel de, 92

Chatterjee, Partha, 53, 60, 120n5, 121n19, 122n20

Cherokee, 55, 71, 121n12, 121n15, 124n36. *See also* Indians

Cherokee Nation v. State of Georgia, 71, 121n12, 121n15

Chicana/o Studies, 125n2

Child, Lydia Maria, 51, 79, 119n1

Chimmie Fadden (Townsend), 21

Christian Union, 67

citizenship of Indians, 69–71, 72, 84, 120n5

Civil Rights Act (1866), 71
Civil War: and abolitionism, 26–27, 65; *Century Magazine* series on, 5, 114n7; commemorations and monuments to, 6; and crisis of national identity, 5, 8, 58; and James, 23, 28–29, 38; military promotion for Ruiz de Burton's husband during, 126n10
civitas, 74
The Clansman (Dixon), 7–10, 114nn10–11
Clinton, Catherine, 32, 118n8
colonial difference: in California, 85–88; Chatterjee on, 53, 121–22nn19–20; dismantling of, 112; and feminist movement, 54; and Indian reform movement, 53–56, 59–61; in Jackson's *Ramona*, 81, 85–86; in Ruiz de Burton's *The Squatter and the Don*, 86–89; and white women's role, 83
colonial governance, 60–61, 120n5
colonial mimicry, 59–60, 82–84
colonialism. *See* imperialism
Columbia University, 117n4
Compromise of 1850, 4–5
The Confidence-Man (Melville), 66
A Connecticut Yankee in King Arthur's Court (Twain), 15–18
consent/force dichotomy, 126–27n17
Constitutional amendments. *See* specific amendments
convict lease system, 90
Conway, Moncure Daniel, 122n22
Cooper, James Fenimore, 10, 12, 119n2
Coronel, Don Antonio, 86
Crawford, Kathleen, 126n10
Creole nationalisms, 10, 11, 115n14, 116n17, 125n6, 128n1
Crook, George, 67
Cuba, 113n2, 129n3
Cultures of United States Imperialism (Kaplan and Pease), 113n3, 119–20n3

Daisy Miller (James), 29, 119n15

Dana, Richard Henry, 125n3
Darwin, Charles, 122n26, 127n20
Davis, Pauline Wright, 32
Dawes Act, 123n33, 124n36
De la Luz Montes, Amelia María, 125n4
DeForest, John, 6
Deloria, Philip, 118n11, 123n30
dialect: in Jackson's *Ramona*, 57–58; James on novel of dialect, 21–26, 28–29; James's refusal of, as literary strategy, 18, 28–29, 34–35, 49; in Twain's *The Adventures of Huckleberry Finn*, 23–24
Dixon, Thomas, 7–10, 114nn10–11
Dodge, Richard Irving, 117n7
domesticity: and assimilation of Indians, 58, 83–84, 123–24n33; feminists versus Victorian ideal of, 32, 49; and frontier, 79–79; and gender division of labor, 8–9, 83–84; and imperialism, 3, 52–57, 82–84, 113–14nn4–5, 119n2; and Indian reform movement, 51–53, 58–59, 65, 83–84; and Indian reform novels, 50–53, 56–60, 76–77, 83; Jackson's *Ramona* and Indian domestication, 72–77, 85; Manifest Domesticity, 52–57, 72, 81, 120n4, 120n7; of Mission Indians, 72, 74–76; and writing, 61–62
Dominican Republic, 113n2
Don Quixote (Cervantes), 92
Dred Scott case, 121n12
Du Bois, E. C., 118n8
Du Bois, W. E. B., 27, 28, 100, 115n12
Dundy, Elmer, 67–68, 122n25
Dunning, William, 117n4

education of Indians, 76–77, 83, 84, 122n21
Eliot, T. S., 22
Elk, John, 70
Elk v. Wilkins, 70
Elliott, Maud Howe, 6
Ellis Island, 36
Emerson, Ralph Waldo, 117n4
empire. *See* imperialism

English language: and immigrants, 44–45; James on, 43–49; pronunciation and enunciation of, 43–46; Webster on American language, 117n4; and whiteness, 43–44, 49; and women's speech, 42–49. *See also* dialect
ethnology, 123–24n33
The Europeans (James), 29

family. *See* marriage
feminist movement: and colonial difference, 54; and imperialism, 82–84, 120–21n10; in James's *The Bostonians*, 19, 27, 31–35, 46–47, 118n7; Manifest Domesticity and feminist studies, 120n4; relationships between racialized populations and feminists, 117n5; and romance of reunion, 31–35; scholarship on, 118n8; and suffrage movement, 123n31; versus Victorian ideal of domesticity, 32, 49
Fiedler, Leslie, 115n15
Fifteenth Amendment, 32
Fletcher, Alice, 123–24n33
Follini, Tamara L., 118n12
A Fool's Errand (Tourgée), 61
force/consent dichotomy, 126–27n17
Foucault, Michel, 122n26, 125n5
foundational fictions, 10–12, 115n13, 125n6
Fourteenth Amendment, 68, 70, 71
Frank Leslie's Illustrated Newspaper, 118n10
Franklin, Benjamin, 62
Freedman, Jonathan, 23
freedmen. *See* blacks
"The Freedmen's Case in Equity" (Cable), 15, 116n18, 121n16
French Revolution, 9
Freud, Sigmund, 122n26
frontier, 1, 67, 79–79, 117n4, 123n29

Gates, Merrill Edward, 77

gender: and blushing, 96–97; and discourse of separate spheres, 51–52, 83; division of labor based on, 8–9, 83–84, 104, 105–6; in James's *The Bostonians*, 30, 33–35. *See also* feminist movement; women
Geronimo, 67
Gerwal, Interpol, 121n10
Gilder, Richard, 5, 30
Gillman, Susan, 112, 129n6
Gilroy, Paul, 112
Glimpses of Three Coasts (Jackson), 75, 86, 93
Goldman, Anne E., 124–25n1, 125n4
Graham, Wendy, 42
The Grandissimes (Cable), 5, 12–16
Grant, Ulysses S., 113n2
Gray, Horace, 70
Greaser Act (1855), 93
Griffin, Susan, 41, 118n13
Griffith, D. W., 114n11
Griswold del Castillo, Richard, 120n9
Guam, 83
Gutiérrez-Jones, Carl, 111, 126–27n17

Habberton, John, 6
Hale, Sarah Josepha, 54, 114n5, 120nn7–8
Harlan, John Marshall, 70–71
Harper's Weekly, 23
Harris, Joel Chandler, 23, 24
Hawaii, 113n2
Hawthorne, Nathaniel, 11, 30
Heizer, Robert F., 125–26n8
Hemingway, Ernest, 23
The Hidden Power (Tibbles), 50–51, 52, 122n23
Higham, John, 118n9
historical alterity, 87–88, 112
historical romances, 3–7, 10, 11, 107. *See also specific authors and their works*
Hobsbawm, Eric, 116n1
Homestead Act (1862), 94
homosocial narratives, 10–12
Houses and House-life of the Ameri-

can Aborigines (Morgan), 72, 123*n*28
Howells, William Dean, 25–26
Hoxie, Frederick, 62, 122*n*21
Huckleberry Finn (Twain), 1–3, 10, 12, 23–24, 115*n*15, 123*n*30
Hudson River School painters, 41
Hurtado, Albert L., 128*n*29

immigration, 35–38, 40, 42–45, 118*nn*9–10
imperialism: in antebellum period, 4–5, 113*n*2; and Berlin Conference (1885), 116*n*1; and Cable's *The Grandissimes*, 12–16; and colonial governance, 60–61; and colonial mimicry, 59–60, 82–84; cultures of U.S. imperialism, 3, 113*n*3, 119–20*n*3; and Dixon's novels, 9–10; and domesticity, 3, 52–57, 82–84, 113–14*nn*4–5, 119*n*2; examples of, 113*n*2; and feminism, 82–84, 120–21*n*10; Hobsbawm on, 116*n*1; and Indian reform movement, 52–53; and James on novel of dialect, 21–26, 28–29; and Louisiana Purchase, 4; and Manifest Destiny, 2–5, 20, 51, 53–54, 66–67, 113*n*1, 119*n*2, 125*n*3; and Manifest Domesticity, 53–57, 81, 120*n*4, 120*n*7; and Twain's *A Connecticut Yankee in King Arthur's Court*, 15–18; and Twain's *The Adventures of Huckleberry Finn*, 115*n*15; and U.S.-Mexican War, 4–5, 54, 92, 113*n*2; and U.S.-Spanish War, 10, 23, 83, 104, 113*n*2. *See also* colonial difference; post-Reconstruction national allegory
In Our Regiment (Rogers), 6
Indenture Act (1850), 90, 125–26*n*8
Independent, 74
India, 120*n*5, 121*n*10, 122*n*20, 127*n*20
Indian agents. *See* reservation system
The Indian Before the Law (Pancoast), 69–70, 80

Indian captivity narrative, 58, 64
Indian Office, 121*n*33
Indian reform movement: and anthropological theories of civilization, 56, 59, 72–74, 83; and assimilation, 58–60, 83–84, 121–22*n*33; beginning of, 56; and Child, 51, 79, 119*n*1; and citizenship of Indians, 70–71, 72, 84, 120*n*5; and colonial difference, 53–56, 59–61; compared with abolitionism, 51, 65–66; and court cases on Indians, 67–71, 121*n*12; and domesticity, 51–54, 58–59, 65, 83–84; and Jackson, 19, 55, 62–65, 77–78, 122*n*22; leadership of, 52; limits of, 77–82; moral appeal of, 66, 83; novels supporting, 50–54, 56–58, 61–82; organizations of, 52, 77, 83; and Ponca flight, 67–69; and Progressive movement, 119*n*1; and U.S. policy on Indians, 55–57, 59, 65, 67–71, 84; and U.S. recognition of tribal sovereignty, 55, 56–57, 69–71. *See also* Indians; *Ramona* (Jackson)
Indian Rights Association, 52
Indian Territory, 1–2, 67, 121*n*30
Indian Trade and Intercourse Act (1834), 2
Indians: and anthropological theories of civilization, 56, 59, 72–74, 83; anti-slavery movement inclusive of, 119*n*1; assimilation of, 57–60, 83–84, 121–22*n*33; and Cable's *The Grandissimes*, 14–15; citizenship of, 70–71, 72, 84, 120*n*5; civilization of Mission Indians, 72, 74–76; court cases on, 67–71, 121*n*12; Deloria on anti-modernist deployment of figure of, 118*n*11; Dodge on, 119*n*7; domestication of, and Jackson's *Ramona*, 71–76, 85; education of, 76–77, 83, 84, 122*n*21; extermination versus civilization of, 55–57, 57–59, 82; Hudson River School painters' depiction of, 41; and Indian Wars, 66–67; Jackson's *A Cen-*

tury of Dishonor on, 62–65, 74, 75, 76; Jackson's early attitude toward, 64; and James's *The American Scene*, 38; Jefferson on, 115*n*16; and kinship, 73–74; as labor force in California, 77, 82, 89–92, 125–26*nn*7–9, 128*n*29; legal status of, 66, 67–71, 90; massacre and Indian captivity narratives on, 58, 64; military defeat of, 55, 58, 66–67, 79; and Ponca flight, 67–69; and property ownership, 76–77, 80–81; qualifications for tribal membership of, 124*n*36; reservation system for, 66, 67, 69, 122*n*23, 124*n*36; in Ruiz de Burton's *The Squatter and the Don*, 99, 104–7; and Spanish and Mexican land grants in California, 86; Spanish colonial Indian policy, 78; Spanish Missions for, 19, 75–76, 89; subjugation of, 4; in Tibbles's *The Hidden Power*, 50–52, 52, 122*n*23; Tourgée on, 107–9, 109; treaties between U.S. government and, 55, 56, 62, 67, 69, 121*n*13; and Twain's *A Connecticut Yankee in King Arthur's Court*, 17, 18; and Twain's *The Adventures of Huckleberry Finn*, 1–2; and Twain's "Tom and Huck Among the Indians," 113*n*1; U.S. policy on, 2, 54, 55–57, 59, 65, 67–71, 84, 121*n*13, 124*n*36; and U.S. recognition of tribal sovereignty, 55, 56–57, 69–71, 121*n*12, 121*n*15; vanishing Indian narrative, 67; white women's domestic influence on, 50–52, 76–77, 83–84, 121–22*n*33. *See also* Indian reform movement; *Ramona* (Jackson)

Irving, Washington, 40–41

Italy, 41–42

Jackson, Andrew, 2, 121*n*13

Jackson, Helen Hunt: *A Century of Dishonor* by, 62–64, 74, 75, 76; early attitude of, toward Indians, 64; *Glimpses of Three Coasts* by, 75, 86, 93; and Indian reform movement, 19, 55, 62–65, 77–78, 122*n*22; investigation of Mission Indians in California by, 74–76; on mestizos, 86; poetry by, 62; and Ponca case, 69; on reservation system for Indians, 66; and romance of reunion generally, 3–4, 19; as Special Agent to Mission Indians, 74–76, 121*n*11; and Stowe's *Uncle Tom's Cabin*, 65–66, 72, 109. *See also Ramona* (Jackson)

James, Henry: and Ashburton Place lodgings in Boston, 38–39; on Athenaeum, Boston, 39–40; autobiography of, 27; Bryn Mawr address by, 45; commercial successes of, 29; deaths of parents of, 47; on dialect, 18–19, 21–26, 28–29, 34, 49; disappearance of former homes of, 39; and Du Bois, 27–28; on Ellis Island, 37; as expatriate, 22, 116*n*2; on food eaten by women, 47–48; on immigration, 35–38, 40, 42–45, 118*n*9; and imperialism and U.S. national identity, 21–26, 27–29, 34–42, 45; on Irving's house, 40–41; on literary novels, 29, 49; on marriage, 48–49; on mass culture, 21–22, 24–25, 27–29; on modernity, 36–42; and race and class, 23, 116–17*nn*3–4; realism of, 23, 34, 116–17*n*3; and romance of reunion generally, 3–4, 6, 11, 18–19; on skyscrapers, 39–40, 43, 118*n*12; on South and Southern, 27–28; and Stowe's *Uncle Tom's Cabin*, 26–28; on women's speech, 42–49. *See also The American Scene* (James); *The Bostonians* (James); *and other works*

James, William, 22, 27–28, 30

James R. Osgood publisher, 30

Jefferson, Thomas, 97–98, 115*n*16

Jim Crow segregation: and black dialect used in literature, 24; Cable on, 15, 116*n*18, 121*n*16; codification of,

2, 7, 17, 66; and discourses of violent black male sexuality, 58; James on, 27–28, 116–17n3; in Twain's *The Adventures of Huckleberry Finn*, 2
Johns Hopkins University, 119n4
The Jungle (Sinclair), 128n25

Kaplan, Amy, 3, 53, 54, 113n3, 114n5, 120n4, 120nn7–8
A Kentucky Colonel (Read), 6
King, Charles, 6
kinship, 73–74
Kipling, Rudyard, 25
Kitty's Conquest (King), 6
Ku Klux Klan, 7–10, 114n11

La Flesche, Francis, 124n33
Lake Mohonk Conference of the Friends of the Indians, 52, 77
Land Act (1851), 94, 95–96, 101
language. *See* English language
The Last of the Mohicans (Cooper), 12
"Last Wave" nations, 115n14
Latin America: anti-colonial thought from, 20, 107, 108–13; historical romances of, 9, 11, 115n13
League of the Iroquois (Morgan), 72
The Leopard's Spots (Dixon), 10
Lewis and Clark Expedition, 13
Liberia, 54, 120nn7–8
Liberia (Hale), 120n7
Lincoln, Abraham, 26, 54, 92, 126n10, 127n24
Lincoln, Mary Todd, 92, 126n10
Lipsitz, George, 127n22
literary realism, 23, 34, 116–17n3
Literature periodical, 21–22
Lomas, Laura, 128n2
Louisiana Purchase, 4, 12–14
Luis-Brown, David, 124–25n1
lynching, 5, 8, 17, 28

Macmillan & Co., 30
Magruder, Julia, 6

Malory, Thomas, 15
Manifest Destiny, 2–5, 20, 51, 53–55, 66–67, 113n1, 119n2, 125n3. *See also* imperialism; post-Reconstruction national allegory
Manifest Domesticity, 53–57, 72, 81, 120n4, 120n7
"The Manners of American Women" (James), 42–43, 47–48
marriage: in Cable's *The Grandissimes*, 12–16; of Californios and Anglos, 19–20, 89, 92–93, 96, 99–101, 126n11; in Jackson's *Ramona*, 58, 63–64, 109–11; James on, 48–49; in James's *The Bostonians*, 19, 33–34; in romance of reunion, 6–8, 11, 12–16; in Ruiz de Burton's *The Squatter and the Don*, 19–20, 89, 92–93, 96, 99, 104–6, 127n23; in Ruiz de Burton's *Who Would Have Thought It?*, 92; in Twain's *A Connecticut Yankee in King Arthur's Court*, 17
Martí, José, 20, 108–13, 128–29nn2–3, 129nn5–6
Marx, Karl, 122n26
Melville, Herman, 10, 66
mestizos: Californios as, 90; Jackson on, 86; in Jackson's *Ramona*, 63, 81–82, 110–12; negative stereotypes of, 87, 125n3; in Ruiz de Burton's *The Squatter and the Don*, 96, 99; sexuality of, 125n3; Tourgée on, 108
Mexican-American War, 4–5, 54, 92, 113n2
Michaels, Walter Benn, 8, 23, 114nn10–11, 116–17nn3–4, 128n28
Miller, David, 113n4
miscegenation, 14 34, 58, 81–82, 92, 99, 110, 116n18
Miss Lou (Roe), 6
Mission Indians, 72, 74–76, 124n35
missionaries and missions, 19, 50–52, 75–76, 89, 119n2
Modern Women anthology, 46
modernity: Foucault on, 125n5; James on, 36–42

Morgan, Lewis Henry, 72–74, 78, 116n19, 122–23nn27–28
Morgan, Matthew, 118n10
Mormonism, 78–79
Morrison, Toni, 22
Morte D'Arthur (Malory), 15
Moylan, Michelle, 124n35
muckraking, 127–28n25

Nation, 38, 46
national allegory. *See* post-Reconstruction national allegory
Native Americans. *See headings beginning with* Indian
"A New England Winter" (James), 46
New Historicism, 125n5
New South, 13, 103, 127n24
New Woman, 3, 49, 114n11
Newman, Louise, 54, 119n5, 120n10
No-Fence Law (1862), 94
North, Michael, 24
North-South relations: and abolitionism, 32; in Cable's *The Grandissimes*, 13–15; and colonial difference, 112; displacement of, by imperialist East-West configuration of national identity, 1–4, 18–20, 85, 107; in Dixon's *The Clansman*, 7–8; and Indian reform movement, 58; James on South and Southern, 27–28; in James's *The Bostonians*, 6, 18–19, 30–31, 33–34, 119n6; and New South, 13, 103, 127n24; and Reconstruction, 1; reunification of, after Reconstruction, 2, 4; and romance of reunion, 6–8; and slavery, 4, 5; in Twain's *A Connecticut Yankee in King Arthur's Court*, 16–17. *See also* abolitionism; Civil War; Reconstruction; romance of reunion; slavery
North American Review, 23, 61
Northwest Ordinance (1786), 4
Notes on the State of Virginia (Jefferson), 97–98, 115n16
novel of dialect. *See* dialect

O'Farrell, Mary Ann, 96–97
Omaha Daily Herald, 68
Omaha nation, 67. *See also* Indians
Osgood, James R., 30
other, 60, 66, 82, 119n2, 125n1
Our Wild Indians (Dodge), 119n7

Padilla, Genaro, 126n12
Page, Thomas Nelson, 23
Pancoast, Henry R., 69–70, 80–81
Peabody, Elizabeth, 30
Pease, Donald E., 113n3
Pequot, 124n36. *See also* Indians
Philippines, 83, 124n34
Phillips, Wendell, 51, 69
Pita, Beatrice, 127n18, 127n23, 128n26
plantation novels, 126n9, 128n28. *See also* slavery
Plessy v. Ferguson, 122n25
"The Point of View" (James), 44
Ponca Nation, 67–69. *See also* Indians
Porfirio Díaz, José de la Cruz, 129n5
The Portrait of a Lady (James), 29, 41–42
Portugal, 116n17
Posnock, Ross, 23, 116n2
post-Reconstruction national allegory: and East-West axis of Twain's *Huckleberry Finn*, 1–3, 12; failure of, 12–18; and foundational fictions, 10–12, 115n13; and homosocial narratives, 10–12; and Indian reform movement, 52–54; in romance of reunion generally, 3–7, 18–20; success of, 7–10; and white supremacy, 7–10. *See also specific authors and their works*
postcolonial theory, 113n3, 120n4
Preemption Act (1841), 94
The Princess Cassimassima (James), 30
Progressive movement, 119n1, 128n28
proletarianization, 20, 88–89, 91, 94, 99, 102, 127n18
property ownership and property crimes, 74, 76–77, 80–81

Prucha, Francis Paul, 122n24
Puerto Rico, 75, 83

The Question of Our Speech (James), 42–45, 48

race. *See* blacks; Indians; Jim Crow segregation; mestizos; slavery; whiteness and white supremacy
racial segregation. *See* Jim Crow segregation
radical alterity, 87, 88, 125n5
railroad: and Jackson's *Ramona*, 124n35; and James, 38, 42, 47; in Ruiz de Burton's *The Squatter and the Don*, 20, 91, 93, 101–7, 127–28n25
Ramona (Jackson): and aesthetics of reform, 61–72; Alessandro Assis in, 58, 63–64, 78–82, 109–11; Alessandro's death in, 64, 80–82; Aunt Ri in, 57, 64–65, 76, 79–81; as bestseller, 57, 124n35; California setting of, 62, 85–86; colonial difference in, 81–82, 85–86; colonial representational practices in narrative of, 61; compared with Ruiz de Burton's *The Squatter and the Don*, 85–88, 124–25n1; dialect in, 57–58; failed national allegory of, 82; Felipe and Ramona's exile to Mexico in, 81, 124n35; first title for, 64; and Indian domestication, 71–77, 85; and Jackson's involvement in Indian reform movement, 55, 62–65; Jackson's purpose in writing of, 63, 65–66; limits of Indian reform movement in, 78–82; love story between Ramona and Alessandro Assis in, 58, 63–64, 109–11; Martí's translation of, 20, 108–13, 128n2; Moreno family in, 63, 78, 86; plot of, 63–64; Ramona as mestiza in, 63, 81–82, 110–12; as romance of reunion, 3–4, 19, 58, 107; serialization of, in *Christian Union*, 67; and Stowe's

Uncle Tom's Cabin, 65–66, 72, 109; Tourgée's review of, 61–62, 107–9, 109
ranchos and rancheros, 89–90, 93–96, 104–7, 126n9
Ransom, Basil, 26–27
rape: of black women, 5, 8, 11, 17; of white women, 8, 58, 122n20
Raphael, Vincent, 124n34
Read, Opie, 6
realism, 23, 34, 116–17n3
Reconstruction, 5, 8, 20, 46, 58, 66, 119n4, 126n8. *See also* post-Reconstruction national allegory
Redeemers, 127n24
reform. *See* Indian reform movement
Renan, Ernest, 34
reservation system, 66, 67, 69, 122n23, 124n36. *See also* Indians
Robinson, Stephen T., 6
Roe, E. P., 6
Roediger, David R., 127n22, 128n27
Rogers, James S., 6
Rogin, Michael, 114n11
romance of reunion: characteristics of, 3–7, 88; examples of, 6; and failure of post-Reconstruction national allegory, 12–18; and feminism, 31–35; marriage in, 6–8, 11, 12–16; and success of post-Reconstruction national allegory, 7–10; and white supremacy, 7–10. *See also specific authors and their works*
The Romance of Reunion (Silber), 6
Romero, Lora, 3, 53, 87–88, 114n5, 119n2, 125n5
Ross, Marlon, 126n15
Ruiz de Burton, María Amparo: California property of, 92; on East Coast, 92; family of, 91; and land speculation, 128n26; marriage of, 92; and military promotion of husband, 126n10; and romance of reunion generally, 3–4, 19–20; *Who Would Have Thought It?* by, 92. See also *The Squatter and the Don* (Ruiz de Burton)
Ryan, Susan M., 119n6

Saldívar, José David, 96
Samoan Islands, 113n2
Sánchez, Rosaura, 127n18, 127n23, 128n26
Sánchez-Eppler, Karen, 53, 119n2, 120n8
Sargent, John Singer, 118n14
The Scarlet Letter (Hawthorne), 11
Schurz, Carl, 55, 76–77
Scribner's Monthly, 12
segregation. *See* Jim Crow segregation
"Self-Reliance" (Emerson), 119n4
separate spheres ideology, 51–53, 83–84
Serra, Father Junipero, 75
sexual division of labor. *See* gender
The Shadow of War (Robinson), 6
"The Significance of the Frontier in American History" (Turner), 1
Silber, Nina, 6–7, 10, 31, 114n9
Sinclair, Upton, 128n25
Sioux, 67. *See also* Indians
skyscrapers, 39–40, 43, 118n12
slavery: in Brazil, 116n17; emotions of slaves, 97–98; James on, 28; and James's *The Bostonians*, 34–35; and Jefferson, 97–98, 115n16; in Latin America, 11, 116n17; legal status of slaves, 66; and North-South conflicts, 4, 5; in plantation novels, 126n9, 128n28; and planter class, 9, 34–35, 126n9; in Twain's *A Connecticut Yankee in King Arthur's Court*, 16, 17; in U.S. territories, 4; women's oppression compared with, 31, 35, 118n7. *See also* abolitionism; blacks
Small, Albion, 119n4
A Small Boy and Others (James), 27
Societas, 74
Sommer, Doris, 10, 11, 115n13, 125n6
The Souls of Black Folks (Du Bois), 27–28
"The South as a Field for Fiction" (Tourgée), 122n25
South-North relations. *See* abolitionism; Civil War; North-South relations; Reconstruction; romance of reunion; slavery

Spanish-American War, 10, 23, 83, 104, 113n2
"The Speech of American Women" (James), 42–49
speech of women, 42–49
The Squatter and the Don (Ruiz de Burton): blushing in, 96, 99–100, 127n20; Californio land dispossession in, 93–96, 100, 101; challenges to racial hierarchies in, 86–88; Chapo in, 104–6; Chicana/o Studies readings of, 125n2; colonial difference in, 86–89; compared with Jackson's *Ramona*, 85–88, 124–25n1; Darrell and Alamar families in, 88–95, 99–102, 104–6, 127n23; decline of Californios in, 88–91, 93–96, 99, 101, 103; failing national allegory in, 88–91; Gabriel Alamar in, 88–91, 100, 101, 128n27; historical alterity of, 88; Indians and blacks in, 99, 104–7; marriage in, 19–20, 89, 92–93, 96, 99–101, 104–6, 127n23; proletarianization of Californios in, 20, 88–89, 91, 94, 99, 102, 127n18; publication date of, 92; railroad in, 20, 91, 93, 101–5, 127–28n25; Redeemer called for at end of, 101, 127n24; as romance of reunion generally, 3–4, 19–20, 107; whiteness of Californios in, 19–20, 87, 89–91, 96, 99–101, 105–7, 124–25n1, 127n17
Standing Bear, 67–69
Standing Bear v. Crook, 67–68
Stokes, Edith, 118n14
Stokes, I. N. Phelps, 118n14
Stowe, Harriet Beecher, 26–28, 54, 65–66, 72, 109, 114n5, 120n8
"A Study in Civilization" (Tourgée), 61–62, 107–9, 109
suffrage, 32, 121n31
Supreme Court, U.S., 70–71, 95, 120n9, 121n12, 121n15, 122n25, 126n12

Telling Complexions (O'Farrell), 96–97
Thanksgiving holiday, 54

Thirteenth Amendment, 101, 126n15
Tibbles, Thomas Henry, 50–52, 52, 68, 69
"Tom and Huck Among the Indians" (Twain), 113n1
Tourgée, Albion, 1, 61–62, 107–10, 122n25, 128n1, 129n5
Townsend, Edward, 21
Treaty of Guadalupe Hidalgo, 90, 93, 97, 120n9, 126n11, 126n16
Trilling, Lionel, 22, 116n2
Turner, Frederick Jackson, 1, 119n4, 121n29
Twain, Mark, 1–3, 10, 12, 15–18, 23–24, 113n1, 115n15, 121n30
Two Years before the Mast (Dana), 125n3

Uncle Tom's Cabin (Stowe), 26–28, 54, 65–66, 72, 109, 120n8
U.S.-Mexican War, 4–5, 54, 92, 113n2
U.S.-Spanish War, 10, 23, 83, 104, 113n2

vagrancy laws, 90
Vallejo, Mariano Guadalupe, 95, 126n9, 126n12
Vallejo, Pláton, 95
Vallejo, Salvador, 126n9
vanishing Indian narrative, 67. *See also* Indians

wage slavery, 128n27
Wald, Priscilla, 55, 121n12, 121n15
Walker, William, 113n2
A War-Time Wooing (King), 6
Ward, Mary Augusta, 25
Wardley, Lynn, 33, 119n15
Warren, Kenneth, 23, 26, 116n3
Washington Square (James), 30
Webster, Noah, 119n4
Wexler, Laura, 53, 119n2
white slavery, 128nn27–28
white women. *See* women
whiteness and white supremacy: and blushing, 97–100, 103, 104; in Cable's *The Grandissimes*, 13–15;
and civilization, 82–83; Du Bois's "wages of whiteness," 100, 101, 115n12; and English language, 43, 49; and idealization of planter-slave relationship, 24; and Indian reform novel, 84; and Jackson, 122n22; in Jackson's *Ramona*, 80, 81; and James, 22, 43, 49, 116–17nn3–4; in James's *The Bostonians*, 19, 34–35; and Jim Crow segregation, 116n18; and Manifest Domesticity, 53–55, 81; and post-Reconstruction national allegory, 7–10, 103; and Reconstruction, 5; and romance of reunion generally, 7–10; in Ruiz de Burton's *The Squatter and the Don*, 19–20, 87, 89–91, 97, 99–101, 105, 124–25n1, 127n17; and women's speech, 49. *See also* Jim Crow segregation
Who Would Have Thought It? (Ruiz de Burton), 92
Wilson, Benjamin Davis, 75–75, 76
Wilson, Woodrow, 119n4
women: access to public social agency for, 51, 54–56, 83, 119n2; domestic influence of, on Indians, 50–52, 76–77, 83–84, 121–22n33; food eaten by, 47–48; and gendered division of labor, 8–9, 83–84, 104, 105–7; imagined native male savagery against white women, 8, 58, 122n20; and Indian reform movement, 50–54; James on preeminence of, 19, 46–47, 48; James on speech of, 42–49; James's address to Bryn Mawr graduating class, 45; Ku Klux Klan and white women, 8–9; and New Woman, 3, 49, 114n11; oppression of, compared with slavery, 31, 35, 118n7; protection of white women, 8; rape of black women, 5, 8, 11, 17; and separate spheres ideology, 51–53, 83–84; suffrage for, 32, 121n31. *See also* domesticity; feminist movement; rape
Women's National Indian Association, 52, 83
women's rights. *See* feminist movement

www.ingramcontent.com/pod-product-compliance
Lightning Source LLC
Chambersburg PA
CBHW031631160426
43196CB00006B/374